The Roses

Στέφον δύ με καὶ λυρίζω,
Παρὰ σοῖς Διόνυσε, σηκοῖς,
Μετὰ Κύρης βαθυκόλπω,
Ῥοδίνοισι ςεφανίσκοις,
Πεπυκασμένος χορεύσω.

Anacreon Ode V.

The Roses

The Complete Plates

PIERRE-JOSEPH REDOUTÉ

1759–1840

TASCHEN

HONG KONG KÖLN LONDON LOS ANGELES MADRID PARIS TOKYO

Contents

PETRA-ANDREA HINZ

Redouté and the Culture of Roses

Pierre-Joseph Redouté was born on 10 July 1759 in St Hubert near Liège in an area of the Ardennes. He came from a family of painters. Churches and monasteries commissioned works from his grandfather, Jean-Jacques Redouté (1687–1752), and his father, Charles-Joseph Redouté (1715–1776) also earned his living as a painter. The three sons thus had an early introduction to art. The oldest son, Antoine-Ferdinand (1756–1809), was a scene painter at the Théâtre italien in Paris; the youngest son, Henri-Joseph (1766–1852), later worked as an artist at the Muséum national d'Histoire Naturelle in Paris, as did Pierre-Joseph. Pierre-Joseph, however, was barely 15 years old when he left his father's care and, as was customary in those days, set out on his travels. He journeyed through Holland, Belgium and Luxembourg and accepted various commissions: interior decorations, portraits and religious works. He became familiar with the works of the great Flemish masters. The flower pictures of Rachel Ruysch (1664–1750) and Jan van Huysum (1682–1749) in particular opened up a new world to him.

In 1782, Pierre-Joseph Redouté went to Paris, where, together with his brother Antoine-Ferdinand, he worked as a stage designer for the Théâtre italien. In his spare time, however, Redouté painted plants. In his constant quest for new subject matter, he discovered the Jardin du Roi, which is now the Muséum national d'Histoire Naturelle. In addition to its zoological and botanical collections, it also ran courses in zoology, botany and mineralogy. The professor for biological iconography at the Jardin du Roi was Gerard van Spaendonck (1746–1822), a Dutchman whose flower engravings are some of the very finest. He noticed Redouté, made him his assistant and had a considerable influence on his artistic development. From van Spaendonck, Redouté learnt the technique of watercolour painting on parchment and also produced plant portraits for the Royal Picture Collection, the Vellum Collection, which now contains more than 6500 watercolour paintings of plants and animals.

At van Spaendonck's suggestion, the professoriate decided to appoint, in addition to an extra botany painter, two further artists for zoo-logical illustrations, to cope with the institution's extended range of tasks and the increased demands of science. The two brothers, Pierre-Joseph and Henri-Joseph Redouté, were chosen, together with an animal painter, so the two brothers were now both at the museum as scientific draftsmen, the older one to paint plants, the younger fish and reptiles. During his time at the Jardin du Roi, Pierre-Joseph Redouté came to know the wealthy amateur botanist, Charles-Louis L'Héritier de Brutelle (1746–1800). L'Héritier cultivated new foreign plants in his gardens in Paris and Picardy and published his descriptions at his own expense in works such as *Stirpes novae* ("New plants", 1785–1805). While looking for a suitable illustrator for his works, he noticed the young Redouté's drawings in the Jardin du Roi and recognised his great talent. While L'Héritier offered him the promise of a regular income, Redouté turned his back on the Théâtre italien and devoted all his energies to painting plants. L'Héritier instructed Redouté in plant anatomy, showed him the morphologically important characteristics of the plants and allowed him to use his large private library. On the basis of the botanical knowledge he acquired from L'Héritier, Redouté was able for the first time to make his pictures scientifically exact. In his early creative period, it is the academic, very naturalistic, botanical but still extremely valuable representation that prevails over any aesthetic demands.

In 1787, Redouté came with L'Héritier to London. Together with the English plant painter James Sowerby (1757–1822), Redouté drew the illustrations for L'Héritier's *Sertum Anglicum* ("English floral wreath", 1789–1792) at the Botanical Gardens in Kew near London. While there, he also learnt about single plate colour printing, which, unlike the French colour engraving process that requires three or four plates, uses only one plate with several colours. Back in France, through L'Héritier, Redouté came to know the horticulturist and botanist Jacques-Martin Cels (1743–1806), from whose garden many of the plants described for the first time by L'Héritier and illustrated by Redouté. Cels also provided a link with Jean-Jacques Rousseau (1712–1778). Although they never met, in

1805 Redouté illustrated Rousseau's *La Botanique* with 65 exquisite plant portraits. In 1788, the royal house finally became one of his patrons when Marie-Antoinette (1755–1793) appointed him as *Dessinateur du Cabinet de la Reine* and granted him access to the Petit Trianon. During the turmoil of the Revolution, which began soon thereafter, Redouté continued to work undisturbed, sometimes on several projects at once.

The first work for which Redouté made all the illustrations himself and obviously also engraved all the plates himself, was *Plantarum historia succulentarum* ("Succulent Plants", 1799–1832) by Augustin-Pyramus de Candolle (1778–1841). This Swiss botanist, who was at that time a medical student in Paris, wrote the accompanying text to the drawings. He later gained general recognition. He became professor of botany in Montpellier and later returned to his home town of Geneva, where he wrote many botanical works and, until his death, was active in a wide variety of fields that extended way beyond his position as a professor of botany. In *Plantes Grasses*, Redouté used the colour stipple engraving method for the first time. This enabled him to achieve the high standard of botanical illustration that distinguished his main works, *Les Liliacées* and *Les Roses*.

Redouté's most important creative period began when, in 1798/99, Napoleon's first wife, Joséphine, acquired the Malmaison château in Rueil, south of Paris. Joséphine was born in 1763 on the island of Martinique and came to Paris when she was sixteen. After her first marriage was dissolved, she married Napoleon Bonaparte in 1796 and was crowned Empress of France in Paris in 1804. She was passionately interested in botany and horticulture, and the design and layout of the Malmaison château garden became her personal concern. She went to great efforts to collect beautiful and rare plants from all over the world and to cultivate them in her gardens. Thus Malmaison became more of a botanical garden rather than the traditional château gardens. The basis of the planting came from Cels' garden near Paris, which was cultivated scientifically by Etienne-Pierre Ventenat (1757–1808), a cleric, librarian and amateur botanist who later became chief librarian at the Panthéon. Joséphine also procured further plants from market gardens and tree nurseries with no regard for cost. Aimé Jacques Alexandre Goujaud dit Bonpland (1773–1858) also made great efforts to have live specimens sent from the botanical gardens at Schönbrunn (Vienna) and Schönfeld (Berlin). Bonpland was a doctor, botanist and explorer. When he accompanied Alexander von Humboldt (1769–1859) on his South American journey (1799–1804), he collected over 4500 varieties of plants, of which 3600 were new to cultivation. On his return, he became Joséphine's private botanist at Malmaison.

These immense efforts made it possible to build up a collection, unique at that time, of plants from outside Europe in just a few years at Malmaison. Joséphine's aim, however, was not just to lay out a beautiful garden, but also to cultivate the collected varieties scientifically. To do this, she appointed Charles-François Brisseau de Mirbel (1776–1854) as horticulturist and secured the co-operation of the renowned botanists, Ventenat and Bonpland, together with the flower painter Redouté, to whom she paid a generous annual salary. Ventenat's diagnostic descriptions are often provided with valuable notes. This gave rise to a magnificent, large format work, *Jardin de Malmaison* (1803–1805), with 120 plates from watercolours by Redouté. When Ventenat died, Bonpland completed the work and published it under the title *Description des plantes rares cultivées à Malmaison et à Navarre* (1812–1817). It contains 55 colour engravings from watercolours by Redouté. The other illustrations are by Pancrace Bessa (1772–1835), another pupil of Gerard van Spaendonck.

Under the patronage of Empress Joséphine, the book on *Liliaceae* was published from 1802 to 1816 in eight volumes with 603 illustrations. The title is misleading, since a broad selection of monocotyleds, such as *Iridaceae*, *Commelinaceae*, *Amaryllidaceae* and *Orchidaceae*, were also represented. The plant descriptions in Volumes 1–4 again were written by Augustin-Pyramus de Candolle. The accompanying texts for Volumes 5 and 6 are by François de la Roche (1780–1813), while those for Volumes 7 and 8 are by

Alire Raffeneau-Delile (1778–1850). With 486 colour engravings, all produced from Redoutés own watercolours, the *Les Liliacées* is his most comprehensive work.

Joséphine's special interest, however, was roses. She was in constant contact with the most important European rose growers and breeders and had a rose garden laid out with the intention of growing all known varieties of rose there. When Empress Joséphine died in 1814, the garden contained around 250 rose varieties. Thus Redouté's rose book also contains a great many roses from the garden at Malmaison, although Redouté and Thory also state that they had obtained roses from the gardens around Paris and from a great many different horticulturists and botanists. The rose book enjoyed immediate success. It contains 170 colour prints using Redouté's particular colour engraving technique. The accompanying text was written by Claude-Antoine Thory (1759–1827), a French horticulturist and botanist who also compiled his observations on roses in a rose monograph of his own: *Prodrome de la monographie des espèces et variétés communes du genre rosier* (1820).

The three volumes of Redouté's rose book were published in 30 installments between 1817 and 1824. There was a large folio edition of only five copies, which contained a monochrome engraving and a hand-coloured engraving for each rose. The small folio edition was printed at the same time. The roses painted by Redouté in this edition can be grouped into three categories: wild roses known to the ancients, such as the dog rose and the evergreen rose; roses from medieval times, such as the white rose and the eglantine rose; and the newer roses, which were appearing when the book was written, with the introduction of the Asiatic roses. Redouté's rose monograph also enjoyed immediate success and had to be reprinted shortly after it first appeared.

The Bourbons were able to form a close connection with Redouté. In 1825, Charles X appointed him Knight of the Légion d'Honneur. Marie-Amélie, the wife of Louis-Philippe, her sister and his daughter were all introduced to flower painting by Redouté, as was Marie-Caroline, Duchesse de Berry (1798–1872), under whose auspices the rose book appeared. In 1822, he followed van Spaendonck to the Muséum national d'Histoire Naturelle, not as professor for biological iconography, but merely as an ordinary, poorly paid teacher of drawing. After the July Revolution of 1830, he became *Peintre de fleurs du Cabinet de la Reine* for the new French queen, Marie-Amélie (1782–1866). In his last productive years, he published two more important works of botanical illustrations: firstly *Choix des plus belles fleurs* (1827–1833), which included 144 illustrations, and in 1836 a selection of 60 new roses (*Choix de soixante roses dédiées à la reine des Belges*).

In conclusion, it should be emphasised that Redouté's personal life was barely affected by the political and social unrest of the time. He survived the difficult years of the Revolution and the Restoration and found approval with the all the rulers who changed in quick succession. Redouté illustrated approximately 50 botanical books, but did not, however, publish any plant descriptions himself. Nor did he create a herbarium. A few examples from the Malmaison garden that served as subjects for his drawings can still be found in Paris today. He died on 20 June 1840, almost 81 years old, and was buried at the Père Lachaise cemetery in Paris.

ROSES IN BOTANY

Rosaceae is a large family of woody and herbaceous plants spread practically throughout the world, but concentrated more in the temperate regions of the northern hemisphere. The family includes many plants grown for their edible fruits: apple, cherry, plum and peach trees, raspberries, blackberries and strawberries. There are deciduous and evergreen trees, bushes and herbaceous plants, but few lianas and no aquatic plants. Important morphological features are alternate, simple or compound leaves, which usually have auxiliary leaves. Nectaries also occur outside the blooms. The blooms are mostly insect-pollinated, large and striking, and normally have five sepals and five separate petals, with numerous stamens and carpels.

2

ROSES IN PALAEOBOTANY

In geological time, roses – meaning the *Rosa* genus as a whole – can be traced back to the Tertiary period (65–2 million years ago). Palaeontologists have found the remains of plants that can be assigned to the genus *Rosa* in the Far East, North America and also in Europe. Fossil finds thus identify the rose as being one of the oldest dicotyledons. However, it is rare to find a rose fossil. The reason for this probably lies in the site requirements of roses, which have remained more or less unchanged to the present day. Roses have never occurred in wet and marshy sites and prefer drier regions where there is practically no chance of plant parts being preserved. Leaf parts, prickly twig remains and, more rarely, flower buds have been found as tertiary rose fossils, but no one has ever found a fossilised flower.

THE ROSE GENUS

Depending on the opinion of different authors, the genus *Rosa* L. comprises one hundred to two hundred species. It is very difficult to identify a species, and here expert botanical opinion often varies widely, since the species are very variable and hybridise easily, meaning that many hybrids arise naturally.

Roses are mainly deciduous, rarely evergreen, erect or climbing shrubs, in other words they produce several shoots from the base, which produce further side shoots. The branches are more or less bristly and prickly. These prickles are sharp, pointed outgrowths of the bark tissue, which is why, unlike true thorns, they are easy to break off. They act as holdfasts and are very important for the reliable identification of a species. Other forms of weaponry are soft, flexible spiny bristles, glandular bristles, which have a spherical gland at their tip, and stem glands. The leaves are alternate, imparipinnate, in other words they have a terminal partial leaf and auxiliary leaves. The leaves are rarely simple, as is the case with the Persian rose, for example. The auxiliary leaves are small, leaf-like structures on each side of the leaf base and are usually attached to the leaf stalk. The flow-ers are solitary or borne in corymbs at the ends of short lateral branches. The inflorescences of wild or species roses are arranged singly, in threes or very occasionally in fives. Garden roses can bear large clusters or panicles of flowers with up to a hundred blooms on one stem. Each individual flower has five sepals, five petals, numerous stamens and many pistils. Modification of the stamens and pistil into petal-like structures produces double-flowered garden roses. Garden roses with five to ten petals are defined as single; those with ten to twenty petals are considered to be semi-double; and those with more than twenty petals are referred to as fully double. The calyx is an elongated structure that unites the ovary and the other reproductive organs. The individual sepals display characteristics that make it easy to identify a species or variety. It is not only their shape (for example simple or pinnatifid) and their size (especially in relation to the petals) which are important, but also how long they persist while the fruit ripens and their position (erect or arched downwards). The five petals of the wild roses are usually broadly rounded, rounded or broadly oval. At the base they have a small attachment, known botanically as a claw. The upper edge of the petals can be rounded or roughly heart-shaped, as can be seen on many of Redouté's illustrations. The flower colour varies from white through pink to red. In Asia, there are even some yellow wild species. Blue does not occur. The fruit develops from the receptacle and is commonly known as a rose hip.

The genus can be further divided into two sub-genera: subgenus *Hulthemia* Focke is distinguished by simple leaves with no auxiliary leaves, and single erect yellow flowers, cf. *Rosa persica* Michaux (p. 30); subgenus *Eurosa* Focke includes the more usual roses with pinnate leaves bearing auxiliary leaves (p. 29, 31 to 197). It is not easy to classify the individual rose groups, including wild species roses, and complete empirical evidence is required to do so.

2 | Distribution of the Genus *Rosa* L.

3 | JOHANN WOLFGANG VON GOETHE (1749–1832)
   The perfoliated rose
   Weimar, Stiftung Weimarer Klassik

3

THE PERFOLIATED ROSE

The phenomenon of flower perfoliation is now called proliferation. It is a deformity, whereby the stem continues to grow through the open flower, usually centrally but occasionally to one side. Whole inflorescences and fruits can also exhibit the phenomenon. Thory and Redouté also observed this morphological phenomenon, but it was Goethe who was particularly preoccupied with it.

Johann Wolfgang von Goethe (1749–1832) was the first to endeavour to understand the various ways in which plants adapt their structure to their surroundings. In 1796 he coined the phrase "morphology", which is still used today in the same sense. He focused his attention primarily on the form of the plant parts and the changes they underwent, paying very little attention to their function as organs. He pursued the idea of a "transcendent primitive plant" which held the original identity of all plant parts. As a hypothesis, he noted down the frequently quoted phrase "everything is leaf". For Goethe's theory concerning the metamorphosis of plants, perfoliation was an especially important piece of evidence. He observed this phenomenon first in a China rose (*Rosa chinensis* Jacq. var. *semperflorens* Koehne). He subsequently found perfoliated roses in various classes of roses, but not in the Centifolia or Provence roses. He did, however, also compile a register of other so-called proliferating plants, including anemones and carnations, for example. In his 1790 *Metamorphose der Pflanzen*, he devoted a whole chapter to the perfoliated rose, which he illustrated with a very attractive watercolour (ill. 3). Redouté drew three perfoliated roses (p. 148, 165 and 174).

WILD ROSES – THEIR DISTRIBUTION AND HABITATS

The natural distribution area of today's roses lies in the northern hemisphere between the 20th and 70th degree of latitude. The *Rosa* genus does not occur in the tropics; nor are there any rose species native to the Southern Hemisphere. The area covered by the genus thus extends over all of Europe, North America and Asia with the exception of the Arctic regions in the north and the tropical regions in the south, together with a few dry regions in inland Asia. The centre of the genus theoretically lies in the mountains of central and south west Asia, but a great variety of forms is also to be found in Atlantic North America. In Africa, roses occur in the wild only in the extreme north west and in Ethiopia (ill. 2).

AMERICAN WILD ROSES

Twenty species of roses grow in the North American region of the United States and Canada. One species (*Rosa montezumae* Humb. & Bonpl., p. 44) is even found as far south as Mexico. One rose with a very large distribution is the Arctic rose (*Rosa acicularis* Lindley). The Japanese rose (*Rosa rugosa* Thunb., p. 40) from the Far East occupies a small area on the south coast of Alaska, making it the hardiest of all rose species.

Roses also occur in California, the Sierra Nevada and the Rocky Mountains. Mention should also be made of the prairie rose (*Rosa setigera* Michaux, p. 177), which is dispersed from the Atlantic right across to the Rocky Mountains and which has often been used in the breeding of winter-hardy climbing roses. In the south, in Texas, Oklahoma and Arkansas, you can find *Rosa foliolosa* Nutét., which is both winter-hardy and very drought-resistant. From the north east come *Rosa blanda* Aiton (p. 46), the freely suckering pasture rose (*Rosa carolina* L., p. 56), the marsh rose (*Rosa palustris* Marshall, p. 63) and *Rosa virginiana* Herrm. (p. 39).

ASIATIC WILD ROSES

Since the distribution centre of the genus *Rosa* L. is to be found in Central Asia, it is difficult to isolate a single typical example to illustrate the Asiatic rose. There are, however, groups of species that occur only or almost exclusively in China, such as the following examples: the Bengal rose group; the Banksian rose group; the smooth-stemmed rose group; the Macartney rose group.

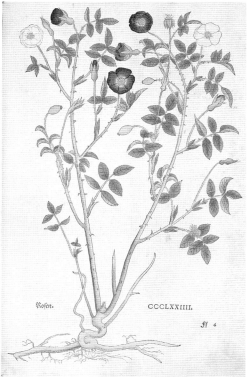

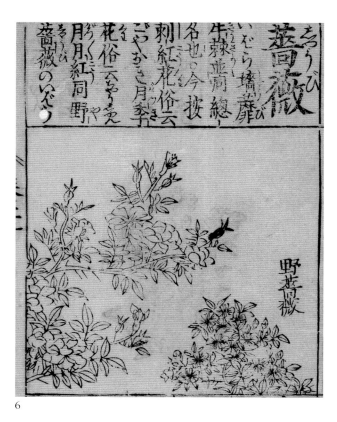

4
5
6

The China or Bengal rose (*Rosa chinensis* Jacq., p. 163, 173 and 189) grows in thickets and on river banks. The Banksian rose (*Rosa banksiae* Aiton fil., p. 104) is an evergreen shrub with smooth stems. Its finely toothed three- to five-palmate leaves bear bristly auxiliary leaves, which fall away. It is winter-hardy only in the mildest of regions. The Cherokee rose (*Rosa laevigata* Michaux, p. 123) is a vigorous, evergreen climbing rose with thick, hooked prickles. In China, it occurs primarily in rocky areas, and is known in Japan only in its cultivated-form. An important identifying feature displayed by the evergreen Macartney rose (*Rosa bracteata* Wendl., p. 34) is its calyx surrounded by large bracts. It gets its common name from Lord Macartney, who brought this rose back to England from China in 1793.

One species is particularly suited to a tropical climate, namely *Rosa clinophylla* Thory (p. 38) from India and Bangladesh. The other Asiatic species of rose grow mainly in low-lying areas, but also on elevated plains. A few species extend right up to the snow level, while others grow on sand dunes along the coast. They thrive in open countryside, as well as on cliffs and on the banks of ravines and gorges. They often climb up into tall trees. *Rosa gigantea* Coll., for example, can grow to a height of 30m, entirely obscuring even the tallest tree.

Two Japanese species should be mentioned with the east Asiatic roses, since they now play an important role in rose breeding. *Rosa multiflora* Thunb. (p. 116) is a one- to three-metre tall climbing shrub with dense, often smooth branches, which has been widely used for hybridisation. The Japanese rose (*Rosa rugosa* Thunb., p. 40) is a one- to two- metre tall shrub with thick, downy stems that are extremely prickly and bristly. There are now many varieties of this rose in Europe.

The Austrian yellow rose (*Rosa foetida* Herrm., p. 51) is one of the most significant roses from Persia and Asia Minor. It has a rather unpleasant scent and was important for the development of yellow and orange coloured garden roses. It is possible that the musk rose (*Rosa moschata*

Herrm., p. 33) also comes from this region. It has been used as the parent of many shrub roses.

EUROPEAN WILD ROSES

Even if Europe does not have the wealth of species present in Asia and North America, many within the genus *Rosa* do in fact occur. The *Flora Europaea* describes 47 species of rose, which can be divided into three groups: the French rose group; the burnet rose group; the dog rose group.

In Europe, roses are usually hill and mountain plants. They need to be close to woodland and require a nutrient-rich, moist site. In Switzerland, the genuine alpine roses, for example, occur only in the regions of pine forests and do not penetrate any lower. The French rose (*Rosa gallica* L., p. 170) is found in light deciduous woodland and on dry meadows, mainly on chalky soil. The burnet rose (*Rosa pimpinellifolia* L., p. 58), which is also called the Scotch or Scots rose, grows as a low-lying, dense bush with acicular thorns on dunes by the coast. It can, however, also occur inland on limestone and gypsum hills. The dog rose (*Rosa canina* L.) appears in a great variety of forms and grows on the edges of woodland and in thickets. The Arctic rose (*Rosa acicularis* Lindley) is a particularly frost-hardy species that even grows close to the Pole.

ROSES IN HERBALS AND THE BEGINNINGS OF ROSE CLASSIFICATION

When the heliocentric view of the world replaced the geocentric one, botany experienced a fundamental revival. Three German scholars, Otto Brunfels (1488–1534), Hieronymus Bock (1498–1554) and Leonhart Fuchs (1501–1566) compiled herbals, descriptions of plants that were then illustrated with realistic woodcuts. Brunfels' 1532 *Contrafayt Kreuterbuch* contains only a single illustration of a rose, which is probably a damask rose (*Rosa × damascena* Miller).

Bock's *New Kreütterbuch* ... appeared in 1539, but this first edition

7

did not include any plant portraits. These appeared only in the second edition of 1546, which was illustrated with woodcuts. Bock differentiates between "Wild Heckrosen/Hanbüttel" (wild briar roses) and "zam garten Rosen" (tame garden roses), of which he includes six different species, although the same woodcut is used for both chapters. In contrast, his notes on the medicinal properties of the rose are extensive.

Fuchs' book, *De historia stirpium*, published in 1542, the German version being entitled *New Kreüterbuch*, is one of the most important works in botanical literature (ill. 4). This book, which has almost 900 pages, contains 511 woodcuts, with a whole page of illustrations being devoted to each plant. Of the plants described, about one hundred are garden plants, with the remaining being wildflowers, so Fuchs also differentiates within his chapter "On Roses" between the wild (species) roses and the garden roses: "Der Rosen seind zweyerley geschlecht fürnemlich zam und wild. Der zamen so man in den gärten pflantzt seind auch zweyerley weiß un rot: und derselben auch zweyerley gefüllt un ungefüllt." (There are two types of rose, wild and cultivated. The cultivated ones that are planted in the garden are either red or white and have either single or double flowers.)

There is, however, only one illustration for the general description of the roses with the particular comment "Krafft und Würckung" (strength and effect). It shows a French rose (*Rosa gallica* L.). This illustration shows different varieties of the same plant, with single and double flowers. On the coloured woodcut they are red, although the same plant also has another pale pink coloured flower (ill. 5).

The works by these three German botanists acted as a great stimulus to European botany as a whole and there was a sudden spate of herbals. Since the 16th century, the main concern of botanists had been to bring the great diversity of the plant world into a system, making it possible to gain an overall picture. At the same time, the individual species had to be given short, clear names. Clarity of nomenclature was a particular concern of

Caspar Bauhin (1560–1624). In his *Pinax theatri botanici* of 1623, he provides a summary of all known plant species (approx. 6000), of which 37 are roses. This work is not illustrated. With this book, he was the first to make a systematic distinction between genus and species. He divided his "*Rosa*" group into garden roses (*Rosa sativa*) and wild roses (*Rosa sylvestris*). He also made a third subdivision for "Rosa Hierichuntia", the so-called rose of Jericho. This is not actually a rose, but a plant from the crucifer family. He names 17 garden roses and 19 wild roses. For each species, Bauhin also gave the plant names used in early botany.

An important list of roses is also contained in the work *Paradisi in sole paradisus terrestris* (1629) by John Parkinson (1569–1629), an English apothecary, which was subtitled as follows *Or a garden of all sorts of pleasant flowers which our English ayre will permitt to be nursed up*. Twenty-four varieties of rose are described in detail, of which 14 are also illustrated.

The names used by Bauhin were almost entirely adopted by Carl Linné (1707–1778), as is shown by the rose example. With his work, *Species plantarum*, (1st edition 1753), Linnaeus created the binomial system of nomenclature that is still in use today. Under this system, a plant's name comprises two parts, the noun part being the genus name, for example *Rosa*, and the following adjectival part being the species name, for example *canina* (*Rosa canina* – dog rose). This system thus did away with the long phrases that had been in common use until then, such as "Rosa sylvestris vulgaris, flore odorato incarnato", which was the name used by Bauhin for the same plant. In his genus *Rosa*, Linnaeus included twelve different species, ten being from Europe, one from America and one Asiatic species. Linnaeus' influence can still be felt today, since his system is still used. It is internationally agreed that the first recorded name of a plant has the greatest validity, with the first edition of *Species plantarum* counting as the starting point for botanical nomenclature.

8

ROSES IN AN EAST ASIAN HERBAL

As an example of a Far Eastern work mention should be made here of an early Japanese work, the 1666 natural history encyclopedia by the neoconfucian scholar Tekisai Nakamura (1629–1702), entitled "Kinmôzui", which soon made its way to Europe. There is a long tradition of encyclopedic dictionaries in Japan and the first ones came about when the Japanese were beginning to learn about Chinese culture. The work in question, which is in several volumes, contains many pictures of biological interest, such as birds, minerals and approximately 250 plants, including roses. Each woodcut shows both the Chinese character and the Japanese synonym. As is the case with the European herbals, the illustration shows the difference between a wild rose (bottom left) and a garden rose (ill. 6).

ROSES IN EARLY EUROPEAN ILLUSTRATED WORKS

In the 19th century, more illustrated works, including several magnificent botanical works with copious large format illustrations, were written on the rose genus. In Germany, a two-volume illustrated rose book by Carl Gottlob Roessig, Professor of international and natural law in Leipzig and horticultural author (1752– 1805), was published, *Die Rosen, nach der Natur gezeichnet* ... (Roses drawn from nature; 1802–1820), but it did not receive any significant attention in botanical circles. At the beginning of the 19th century, Henry C. Andrews (1770–1830), an English botanist and plant painter, published a monograph on the genus *Rosa*, *Roses*, ... (1805–1828). He also made his own relief plates from his plant portraits, just as Redouté had done for his work on succulent plants. The two volumes contain 129 copperplate engravings, including one of the first tea rose, which he published in 1810 under the name *Rosa indica odorata*.

The rose book that is most relevant in botanical terms was written by John Lindley (1799–1865), another English botanist, who was secretary of the Royal Horticultural Society in London for 40 years and who wrote several botanical works. He was an important scientist and a highly gifted

draftsman and also had a keen interest in plant breeding. His rose monograph, *Rosarum Monographia or a botanical history of roses* (1820), contains a hundred rose descriptions, in which he goes into great detail about the individual plant parts. He illustrated 19 roses with his own drawings, together with the pasture rose from America (*Rosa carolina* L., ill. 7, also p. 56). In the case of some roses, he refers to Redouté's illustration, where there was one. Lindley's rose monograph was used as a reference book for 150 years, even though not all roses can be clearly identified in this work.

GARDEN ROSES

Unlike the wild roses described above, garden roses are developed by man and not by nature. They are a product of controlled breeding and are given variety or cultivar names. A variety describes a stock of cultivated plants that has particular distinguishing features that it retains when propagated vegetatively. To make it easier to get an overview, the huge number of rose varieties are divided into different groups, but today, reflecting the huge gene pool of roses, they are also divided into "old garden roses", "modern garden roses" and the wild roses described above. Each group includes climbing and bush roses.

A rose is described as an "old rose" if it belongs to a rose category (in the horticultural sense) that was in existence prior to 1867. The first crosses with the Asiatic species introduced in the 19th century still come under this group, so all the garden roses drawn by Redouté can be described as "old roses". The phrase "modern roses" was not used until 1867, when the first hybrid tea (large-flowered bush) roses were introduced. In this connection, the lifespan of a rose variety is also significant, in the sense of how long the variety is available on the market. As a general rule, this is not for long, although many of the old roses are already more than 150 years old. They would have died out long ago had not rose growers and enthusiasts continued to cultivate them despite their faults, such as their short flowering period, for example. Nowadays, most rose varieties are on the market for little more than five years before they are replaced by newer, improved varieties.

As cultivated plants, rose varieties are now given names on three main levels: genus, species and variety (cultivar), with variety being the lowest level. The genus and species names are in Latin, while modern languages are used for the variety names, which are shown in single quotation marks ('…').

OLD ROSES

As Rome and its culture declined, so too did the passion for roses. Had it not been for a few monastery gardens, garden roses would scarcely have survived. It was not until the time of Charles the Great (742–814) that people were once again encouraged to grow them, particularly as a medicinal plant. Unlike carnations and particularly tulips, roses at that time did not have an important role to play as ornamental plants. During the Crusades, the French rose (*Rosa gallica* L.) and the damask rose (*Rosa × damascena* Miller) were brought to central Europe, and by 1300 rose growing was already very widespread in France. In the Renaissance, rose growing really took off, as can be seen from the paintings of that period. The white rose (*Rosa × alba* L.) is particularly well represented. It is not a wild species, but a hybrid of disputed parentage. It is not known when this rose, of which there are about 200 varieties, was first cultivated, but it has definitely been in general cultivation since Greek and Roman times. The white rose was widespread in the Middle Ages, particularly in its semi-double form (*Rosa × alba* L. 'Semiplena', p. 74).

The French or Provence rose has been indigenous to most of Europe since the earliest times and was an important economic plant in France, where it was grown for the production of essential oils, especially the apothecaries' rose (*Rosa gallica* L. 'Officinalis', p. 53) with its single red blooms. A variety named 'Versicolor' (p. 83) with carmine red and white striped petals, was even illustrated in the *Hortus Eystettensis* (1613). Gallica

roses began to be cultivated in Holland around 1670. In 1811, Joséphine had 167 varieties in her garden.

It is now thought that damask roses (*Rosa × damascena* Miller) are a natural hybrid of *Rosa gallica* and another rose. The origin of this rose is unclear, but it probably came to central Europe with the Crusaders in the 13th century. The "rose of Paestum" could also possibly be included here. In ancient times, Paestum, which lies south of Naples, was a rose-growing centre famous for its rose gardens. There are varieties of damask roses that flower once (summer-flowering roses: *R. gallica* L. × *R. phoenicia* Boiss.) and those that flower twice (autumn-flowering or remontant roses: *R. gallica* L. × *R. moschata* Herrm.). Even Pliny reported on the remontant rose of Cyrene in North Africa. Because of North Africa's favourable climate, the roses appear to be dormant in January-February and again in July-August, going on to develop flowers in the following months. They were given the botanical name of *Rosa × bifera* Pers., but in France they were called the "Quatre Saisons" (p. 69 and 76). In 1811 there were already four varieties, and by 1848, 100 remontant damask roses were cited. The autumn-flowering damask roses were subsequently crossed with other roses and produced the remontant damask roses. Before breeding began with this rose, there was already a bi-coloured variety (*Rosa × damascena* Miller 'Versicolor', p. 84), known as the York and Lancaster rose, as it appeared after the Wars of the Roses in England (1455–1485) and its flowers combine the colours of the feuding houses of York (white) and Lancaster (red). Unlike the striped Gallica rose, the flowers of the York and Lancaster rose usually display all red or all white petals in one flower.

Provence or centifolia roses (*Rosa centifolia* L.) are complex hybrids that developed gradually from the end of the 16th century to the beginning of the 18th. Between 1710 and 1850, they were developed solely in Holland, where their fully double blooms were arose through mutation. The centifolia rose can be seen on many paintings by Dutch masters. The common moss rose (*Rosa centifolia* L. 'Muscosa', p. 36 and 37) also belongs in this category. This variety was produced by mutation even before 1750. They are called moss roses as they have a mossy growth on the calyx, often in conjunction with prickles and oil glands.

The first breeders were Frenchmen who, in the environs of Paris, received much encouragement from Empress Joséphine. The early varieties were propagated by means of division, layering, hardwood cuttings and occasionally also by means of bud grafting. At the beginning of the 19th century, a French rose breeder created the first new varieties by means of artificial pollination. The extent to which plants were bred systematically or arose through chance cross-pollination between 1810 and 1860 can no longer be verified, but after 1860 only intentional crosses were made.

Apart from an initial development in Holland with the breeding of the centifolia roses, rose breeding did not really start until after the introduction of various species from Asia. The introduction of American roses is insignificant here, since crossing with American wild species did not produce any commercially viable results. Admittedly, the Noisette rose (p. 121) did come from North America to Paris at the beginning of the 19th century, but this was presumably a natural hybrid of *Rosa chinensis* Jacq. and *Rosa moschata* Herrm., so the parent plants are thus of Asiatic origin. Louis Noisette sent a specimen of the new Bengal rose to his brother Philippe in North America. The latter then sent the seeds it produced, together with propagated plants, back to Louis in Paris. A few years later, this rose had become widely distributed and indeed Redouté included it in his rose book.

THE INTRODUCTION OF ROSES FROM ASIA

The forebears of nearly all garden roses come from Asia, and these have been extensively interbred to produce the plants we grow today. Without them, there would be no remontant roses (roses which flower several times in a season), no yellow roses and no climbing roses. Canton was the only city in China to open its doors to international trade in the 16th century. In 1684, the English set up a branch of the East India Company there. A great many plants reached England by way of the company. The Chinese also kept a tree nursery in Canton, and this is where many of the plants sent to Europe came from. Many roses were brought to Europe at the end of the 18th and beginning of the 19th centuries, but it was Ernest H. Wilson (1876–1930) who brought the most. Wilson travelled through China, Japan and Korea between 1906 and 1919 and introduced many valuable plants to garden cultivation.

The China rose (*Rosa chinensis* Jacq.) is important to rose breeding for two reasons: firstly because it is remontant, and secondly because of its red flower colour. Before the introduction of this rose, Europe had no variety with such a deep red flower colour. All dark red roses thus originate from this species. Slater's crimson China rose (*Rosa chinensis* Jacq. var. *semperflorens* Koehne, p. 41, 142 and 176) was discovered by an Englishman in a garden in Calcutta in 1789 and brought back to England. In 1798, it was cultivated by Cels and Thory in Paris. Goethe also knew of this rose and observed proliferation in it.

The tea rose (*Rosa × odorata* Sweet, p. 47) is a very close relative of the China rose, but has larger, more fragrant, semi-double, yellow to apricot yellow blooms and was found in China, where it was already being cultivated. The scent of its petals and its leaves when crushed is said to have been strongly reminiscent of crushed tealeaves. The varieties developed since then have lost their scent, but the name has stuck. They are thought to be hybrids of *Rosa chinensis* Jacq. and *Rosa gigantea* Coll.

The "Île de Bourbon", now Réunion, in the Indian Ocean was an important transhipment port for French ships on the way to the Middle and Far East. It was here that a botanist discovered a new hybrid in a rose hedge planted with both China and damask roses. In 1819, he brought it to France, and from its seed a new rose was developed with semi-double pink flowers and a second flush of flowers in autumn. It was called the Bourbon rose (*Rosa × borboniana* N. Desp., p. 196) and was painted by Redouté in 1822.

9 | STEFAN LOCHNER (1405/15–1451)
Madonna in the Rose Bower, c. 1450
Cologne, Wallraf-Richartz-Museum

9

MODERN ROSES

The remontant roses, which have several flowerings, are considered to be the link between old and modern roses. They set ablaze a real breeding fever in the second half of the 19th century. Its origin is difficult to explain, as all the important groups of garden roses contributed to its development. The largest group of modern garden roses is the large-flowered bushes (hybrid teas), of which more than 6000 varieties have been bred since the end of the 19th century. But constant crossing, inbreeding and the pursuit of particular breeding aims caused the hybrid tea roses to degenerate to a large extent. Their resistance to disease was considerably decreased when it was crossed the Austrian yellow rose (*Rosa foetida* Herrm., p. 51), although this did extend the colour range to include yellow and orange-red tones. The findings of Gregor Mendel (1822–1884) with regard to genetics had a huge impact on the rose breeders' work. His principles were, however, initially ignored, ("Experiments with plant hybrids" was published as early as 1866), and it was not until after the turn of the century, when his findings were rediscovered, that they became accepted in plant breeding. When looking for Mendel's "inheritance factors", scientists discovered chromosomes, and today the genus *Rosa* is one of the most thoroughly investigated plant groups in cytological terms. The extended knowledge of cytology has revolutionised rose breeding to such an extent that there are now over 12,000 varieties, with new ones being introduced each year. They are divided into various groups, of which the most important ones are: grandiflora roses, polyantha roses, cluster-flowered bush roses, miniature roses and climbers of varying origin. All these new rose varieties, however, are very different from Redouté's roses.

ROSES IN MEDICINE

Roses were and still are used both in the West and in the East to produce medicines. Chinese medicine uses primarily the Japanese rose (*Rosa rugosa* Thunb., p. 40) and *Rosa multiflora* Thunb. (p. 116). The dried leaves of the Japanese rose can still be obtained from pharmacies today. In traditional Chinese medicine, the Japanese rose was used to bring down temperature and as a remedy for a dry mouth, excessive thirst, malaria, diarrhoea and external bleeding. Today the Japanese rose has gained the upper hand. In addition to these two roses, the Cherokee rose (*Rosa laevigata* Michaux, p. 123) is used to treat infertility.

In Egypt, roses were considered to be a panacea. They had to import the coveted rose products, such as rose water, from Crete or Cyprus, which had large rose gardens. There were well-known rose gardens even in Ptolemy's time and under the Romans, particularly in Lower Egypt. The roses were used to make rose water and rose balm.

In his "Enquiry into plants", Theophrastus (371–287 BC) mentioned roses, and in his De Materia Medica, which cites all known medications in its five volumes, Dioscorides (1st century AD) devoted a whole chapter to the garden rose. Roses have a cooling and astringent effect. Rose remedies are mentioned for headaches, earache and pain in the eyes, mouth, gums and anus. Pliny the elder (23–79 AD), the Romans' only scientific writer, also emphasises the curative powers of the rose in his natural history. He recommends it for complaints of the spleen and intestines, bleeding, and pleurisy. Rose preparations also played a significant role in Arab medicine, as Avicenna (980–1037) relates. In another source, rose water production is described in various chapters.

In the 12th century, the Palermo school provided a first for Europe when it discovered rose-hip syrup, which is still in use today, and which is good for colds, headaches and reducing temperatures. North of the Alps, roses were grown in monastery gardens and small medicinal or herb gardens as useful, rather than ornamental plants. Thus there were plans to plant roses in the monastery garden in St Gallen (820), and Walafrid Strabo (809–849), abbot of the abbey in Reichenau on Lake Constance, also writes about the rose. Rose preparations were particularly recommended by St Hildegard of Bingen (1098–1179), abbess of the St Rupertsberg cloister

10

at Bingen: "The rose is cold, but this coldness can be used to good purpose. Collect rose petals at dawn and place them over the eyes, they make them clear and draw out the 'sleep'." The 16th century herbal authors adopted Dioscorides' multi-facetted indications and transferred them to the garden roses of that time. A French rose variety (*Rosa gallica* L. 'Officinalis', p. 53), also known as the apothecaries' rose, was the rose most used in medications and there is proof that it was already being cultivated in France in 1310. In Provins, a village south-east of Paris, a centre for cultivating this plant grew up and continued for over 600 years. This is a very fragrant, semi-double, carmine red rose.

The apothecaries of the Middle Ages and of early modern times sold the following rose-based remedies: Rose petals for inflammation of the eyes, gallbladder trouble and as a laxative; Rose vinegar for fatigue and impotence, to make rose vinegar, the dried buds of the apothecaries' rose were steeped in wine vinegar; Rose powder from the dried and crushed flower petals of the apothecaries' rose; Rose seed as a vermicide, although really the hips were intended here; "Bedeguar" galls for insomnia, a tincture made from the dried growths (galls) produced by the rose gall wasp on the branches of the dog rose. In German-speaking countries, these galls were also known as "Schlafäpfel" (sleeping apples); in English they are also known as "Robin's pincushions". Rose water to improve the taste and smell of a medicine. Rose water was made from the flowers of the Provence rose and the French rose; Root bark of the dog rose for rabies-infected dog bites; Rose sugar made from the flowers of the Provence rose and the French rose as a purgative and antipyretic. The most important remedy was undoubtedly rose water, which was already an important commodity in the 8th and 9th centuries and which was not replaced by rose oil until some time later. The fresh fruits of the dog rose are used in medicine as a diuretic, refrigerant and mild astringent. They are also a valuable source of Vitamin C and are used to make rose hip tea and jam.

ROSE SCENT

Since the Ancient Greek and Roman times, people have tried to capture the scent of rose flowers in a usable form. Perfumed ointments were produced by extracting the oils and fats from rose petals. However, it was not possible to isolate the pure essential oil until the Arabs had invented steam distillation. Today, a variety of the damask rose (*Rosa* × *damascena* Miller 'Trigintipetala') is the most important rose for oil production. Around 1700, the Turks introduced oil rose cultivation to the Balkans, but oil rose cultivation spread only to the "Valley of the Roses" in northern Thrace in Bulgaria. Production of "Bulgarian rose oil" in the Anatolian Mountains of Turkey has now outstripped that of its country of origin. At a height of 1000 m, the ecological conditions in these mountains are particularly favourable for growing damask roses. Bulgarian rose oil is used not only in pharmacology and medicine, but also in the perfume and cosmetics industries. In southern France and Morocco, an essential oil is produced from the Provence rose by means of steam distillation. It has a similar composition to Bulgarian rose oil, but does have a different scent. In the perfume town of Grasse in southern France, on the other hand, a hybrid of the Provence and the French rose is used. Since the 13th century, rose water has also been used in the kitchen to flavour sauces, soups and stews. Marzipan and other confectionery are still made using rose water today. It is also used as an additive to some herb-flavoured liqueurs.

ROSES IN ART

Because of its beauty, scent and ephemerality, the rose is usually connected with three spheres of life: love, death and Elysium. According to mythology, the rose grew out of the blood of the dying Adonis. It became a symbol of Aphrodite, and the Romans also attributed it to their goddess of love. Although the rose was extolled as "the queen of flowers" even in early Greek poetry, for example in Sappho's songs of Nature, the pictorial art of the rose seems to have met with less interest. It was not until after the naturalistic

11

decoration of Minoan and Mycenian art that individual motifs, such as the rose, were remoulded into strictly stylised plant forms, such as the rosette. A clear rose bud can however be seen on coins from Rhodes. Roses came to Rome from Greece early on. From the 3rd century BC until the fall of the Roman Empire, the rose is frequently mentioned in literature and also played an important role in the cult of death. Roses can also be found depicted in mosaics, and in frescoes in catacombs, especially in early Christian art. As the Christian church spread across Europe, the rose, which had previously been a symbol of Venus, came to symbolise the martyrs and Christ's Passion. In Roman times, however, roses were portrayed so generally, that it is impossible to identify them with any degree of certainty. In the Middle Ages, the rose becomes the embodiment of love and of spiritual and earthly beauty. It also became the preferred symbol of the Virgin Mary, the white rose representing her humility, the red her love. The red rose is also a symbol of the martyrs.

Artists have highlighted these various levels of significance as a central theme in various pictures: as the Madonna standing by a rose bush or rose-covered sceptre or in the rose-covered Hortus conclusus. In the 15th century, the latter gave rise to the picture type of the Madonna sitting in front of a rose trellis. This symbolism is particularly clear in the devotional pictures *Madonna in the Rose Bower* (ill. 9) by the most important painter of the Cologne School, Stefan Lochner (1405/15–1451), and *Madonna of the Rose Hedge* by Martin Schongauer (1445–1491). Schongauer's painting shows two different roses. The white, semi-double rose is thought to be *Rosa × alba* L. 'Semiplena', the red one *Rosa gallica* L. Roses cut in wood or stone above confessional boxes symbolise secrecy, hence the phrase "sub rosa". This symbolism also explains the *Portrait of a Notary* (ill. 11) by Quentin Massys (1465/66–1530).

Depictions of roses became more frequent in Italian art from about the 15th century and were painted with increasing accuracy. Today, three roses can be recognised from the paintings: the red, single French rose, the white, double White Rose of York and its pink form. *The Birth of Venus* (ill. 8) by the Florentine painter, Sandro Botticelli (1445–1510) is worth mentioning here. The cascading roses can be identified as *Rosa × alba* L. The White Rose of York is depicted in other paintings by Botticelli. The only one of his paintings to show a red rose, probably a French rose, is *La Primavera*.

The Provence and damask roses are depicted in the paintings of the great Dutch and Flemish masters. Jan Bruegel the elder (1568–1625), Rachel Ruysch (1664–1750) and Jan van Huysum (1682–1749) painted many pictures with roses (ill. 10). A work by J. Bruegel the elder, *The Allegory of Scent,* even illustrates how roses were used. It depicts a garden with flowering plants and rose pickers with a laboratory complete with distilling equipment to produce rose water as a medicine. There is a picture by Rachel Ruysch, court painter in Düsseldorf, of an Austrian yellow rose (*Rosa foetida* Herrm.), one of the west Asiatic roses brought to Spain by the Moors. The striped rose (*Rosa gallica* L. 'Versicolor') can also be recognised in the works of Dutch masters, including Redouté's teacher, Gerard van Spaendonck. As we progress through history, the cult of the rose becomes more general, and with the beginning of European garden cultivation the rose increasingly becomes a decorative or ornamental plant as well as a symbol of earthly love.

BARBARA SCHULZ

Redouté: technique and method of printing

"The method for printing plates in colour which we invented in 1796, bears no relation to that which Bulliard employed in his Champignons. *His technique, which was merely an imitation of Le Blon's manner, consisted in the use of different colours on more than one plate for printing each of his subjects.*

Our process, on the other hand, consists of the use of these same colours, on a single plate, by a method unique to us, and which we plan one day to publish. It is by this method that we have succeeded in imparting to our engravings all the softness and brilliance of watercolour, as can be seen in our Plantes grasses, *in our* Liliacées, *and other works."*

Les Roses, volume 1

The popularity of the series *Les Roses* continues to this day thanks above all, to the beauty and delicacy of their true-to-life portraiture by Pierre-Joseph Redouté. It was not until their reproduction by the printer Firmin Didot in Paris that these works could become known to the public at large. The method by which these reproductions were achieved can only be ascertained by a close examination of the prints. The sole clue to the technique used is found in a footnote to the foreword on page ten of volume one. The note is not very instructive, rather more concealing than revealing. The point is made that more than one colour was printed from a single plate. The author is silent on the fact that *all* the flower colours were rendered in watercolour. One cannot, therefore, characterize *Les Roses* as colour engravings. They are two and three colour prints in which the flowers, leaves, and stems, even the prickles have been retouched with watercolour by another hand.

On each of the more than one hundred sixty rose portraits, the legend names Redouté, painter; Rémond, printer, and at the right, the respective engraver. (In this position the designation has conventionally been used for line engraver or etcher.) The harmonious collaboration of so many different engravers can be attributed to their all using the stipple technique of copper engraving. Small, toothed wheels were used, as were needles for the individual dots. Lines were added, but the margins of the leaves and flowers were stippled as well, so that no sharp outlines were created. All shaded parts were built up of dots. In this way, the softness of form was achieved.

Les Roses was published in installments in which some ten different artist/engravers participated; most of them produced several plates. They are in volume one: Bessin, Chapuy, Charlin, Couten, Coutan, Gouten, Langlois, Lemaire; in volume two: In addition to the above, Chardin, Talbeaux, Teillard, Tilliard, Victor; in volume three: Bessin, Bessa, Langlois, Lemaire and Victor.

All engravers' names were cut into the plate by a letter engraver and were always printed in black. The principal engravers are Langlois, with fifty-eight plates, and Chapuy with forty-two plates. Victor, the new engraver whose work first appeared in volume two, is distinguishable from the others by the three dimensional quality of his work and the graphic quality of his leaf rendering. Thus, in many rose species his leaves can appear wrinkled and life-like, whereas they would usually be rendered schematically and undifferentiated. Still, Victor used the same stipple tools and roulettes that the other engravers used.

Once the plates were engraved, a black print was pulled to check the quality of the engraver's work as well as to reduce somewhat the sharpness on the plate. The colour print requires none of the depth of dots and lines that gives the black and white print its richness of contrast; the different colours have already achieved the necessary light and dark tones.

The colouration in the print is limited to those few colours that reproduce the tones of the Original design. These are always green, with added gold ochre or brown tones. In the case of light and bright pink flowers, pink is also rubbed into the plate. This localised inking is called *à la poupée* and was done with fingertips wrapped in muslin for this purpose. Tampons were also used for larger areas of colour.

After the plates were inked, superfluous colour was wiped away and here, too, with muslin-wrapped fingertips in the smaller areas. Thus the colours remained in the cavities of the stippled parts. It was after these preparations that printing took place. The resulting print was a model with green predominant, and small spots of gold brown inserted for the stamens and pistils.

To print several colours from a single plate required a high level of skill on the part of the printer. Since the copper plate contained the entire picture, the printer had to determine afresh, the placing of the individual colours before making the impression. On the other hand, the Le Blon method mentioned in the footnote, calls for the distribution of blue, red and yellow (and sometimes black) inks, each on its own plate on which the corresponding portions of the three colours and where they blend had been prepared by the engraver. The three to four plates were printed one after the other. In Le Blon's method the mezzotint process was used; these were true colour engravings. The method is time consuming though dependable as to results, in contrast to the printing of many colours from a single plate, a process that allows for imperfections and can be executed only by experienced printers. The printers were well aware of their importance, judging by their identification by name on the plate.

In the prints executed by Rémond, who printed all plates, black was not used, except for *Rosa gallica*, *purpurea velutina*, *parva*, engraved by Langlois (p. 91). The black ink was rubbed in locally and blends a little into the green of the stem under the flower. Otherwise, colour was applied to the print in matching tones: printed green under green colouring, light gray or light green as shading tones under the white flowers.

The engravers, despite their number, managed to give the work the appearance of uniformity. This was due in no small part to the skill of the printer, who always worked with the same tones and, in foregoing the use of black, provided the light toned foundation for the important work that followed. His work is consequently vital to the finishing colouration with watercolour. In the footnote cited, Redouté is silent about this procedure. Still, it was the colourist, called at that time, illuminator, who imparted their full colour to the roses. With these colours he completed the botanical fidelity of the representation. The majority of colourists were mostly women who sat together in so-called colouring rooms and carried out the watercolour process according to Redouté's models. Each of the women applied only one thin colour wash; she then passed the sheet to her neighbour who, in turn added another colour, and so on. This method of working produced neat and accurate results. There are no traces of templates to be seen; the work must have been done free hand. Although the printing paper was mostly white, white flowers were also overpainted white. The application of a thin layer of white gives the stippled light green or gray shades their luminescence and softness.

The printing in installments of *Les Roses* extended over seven years: 1817–1824. When one thinks of the number of participating engravers, printers, and illuminators who were so essential to the superb realization of Redouté's drawings, not to mention the important scientific descriptions which the botanist Thory. provided for each specimen, it is small wonder that the enterprise eventually exceeded Redouté's financial resources. Fortunately, with the help of interested patrons, the work could be brought to completion. In view of these difficulties, the uniform quality maintained by the craftsmen is all the more admirable.

12

13

12 | ROSE WREATH
    Charlin, engraver
    Cambridge, USA

13 | ROSE WREATH
    Charlin, engraver
    Göttingen, Universitätsbibliothek

14 | ROSE WREATH
    Ultraviolet reflectography
    Göttingen, Universitätsbibliothek

15 | ROSE WREATH
    Charlin, engraver
    Tübingen, Universitätsbibliothek

The illustrations 12, 13 and 15, show three different copies of the frontispiece illustration for Les Roses; *colour stipple engraving, printed in, at most, three colours: green, gold ochre, and brown. The Greek poem in the center is printed in yellow gold ochre. The legend underneath is in all cases printed in black. A rich colouring, appropriate to the subject is added: several green tones; over brownish printed stamens, yellow colouring; several pink and red tones. Yellow is always coloured, never printed. White roses are always coloured in so that the printed shading is somewhat muted. The illumination is very precise, accomplished without the aid of a template. When one compares the wreaths in the different copies, it becomes apparent that the overpainting conforms precisely to the model. The richness of the overpainting, covering the print completely, becomes visible in the ultraviolet reflectography from Göttingen. Prints produced from worn plates were more intensely coloured (13 and 15). In the Tübingen copy the colouring is very strong.*

14

15

16

16 | ROSE WREATH
      Detail, yellow flower, upper right

17 | ROSE WREATH
      Detail, yellow flower
      Ultraviolet reflectography

18 | ROSE WREATH
      Detail, enlarged

The illustrations show a detail of the yellow blossom at the upper right of the rose wreath from the Göttingen copy. The ultraviolet reflectography shows as well that an overpainting of light yellow lies as a covering colour layer on the print. In the further enlargement the stippling under the yellow colouring is clearly visible.

17

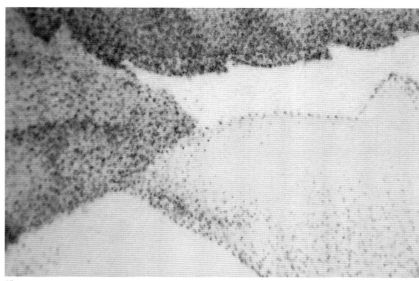

18

19 | ROSA CENTIFOLIA L.
   Couten, engraver

20 | ROSA CENTIFOLIA L.
   Detail of stem

21 | ROSA CENTIFOLIA L.
   Detail of stem, enlarged
   Göttingen, Universitätsbibliothek

The illustration of Rosa centifolia L. *is an example of printing in red for the rendering of flower petals, with an added delicate sheen of watercolour. The stems are printed and coloured. At the point of attachment of the flower stem (21), two separate colours can be seen, side by side, in the hollow produced by the tool — an illustration of printing in more than one colour from a single plate. One sees the stippling well; also, rows of dots, produced by the roulette. In these details from the Göttingen copy the illumination is seen to be very transparent and lustrous; in ill. 20, the inward-curling rose petal has no stippling, only a glossy application of colour.*

19

20

21

22

23

22 | ROSA MUSCOSA
    Leaves, printed and coloured

23 | ROSA MUSCOSA
    Leaves, ultraviolet reflectography
    Göttingen, Universitätsbibliothek

*The ultraviolet reflectography of the Göttingen
copy shows the full colouring of the leaves.*

24 | ROSA EGLANTERIA
    Langlois, engraver. Light yellow

25 | ROSA EGLANTERIA
    Ultraviolet reflectography
    Göttingen, Universitätsbibliothek

Rosa eglanteria *is printed with little colour, with
only yellow and green colouring. The ultraviolet
reflectography shows the thick colouring.*

24

25

The Plates

Rosa centifolia.   *Rosier à cent feuilles.*

P. J. Redouté pinx.   Imprimerie de Remond   Couten sculp.

ROSA CENTIFOLIA L. 'MAJOR'

Cabbage Rose | Zentifolie | Rosier à centfeuilles

Rosa Berberifolia   *Rosier a feuilles d'Epine-vinette.*

P.J. Redouté pinx.   Imprimerie de Rémond   Chapuy sculp.

ROSA PERSICA MICHAUX

Barberry Rose | Persische Rose | Rosier de Perse ❧

Rosa Sulfurea. *Rosier jaune de souffre.*

P.J. Redouté pinx. Imprimerie de Rémond Langlois sculp.

ROSA HEMISPHAERICA HERRM.
Sulphur Rose | *Schwefelrose* | *Rosier à fleurs jaune soufre*

Rosa Rubrifolia.   *Rosier à feuilles rougeâtres.*

P. J. Redouté pinx.   Imprimerie de Rémond   Chapuy sculp.

ROSA GLAUCA POURRET

Red-leaved Rose | *Rotblättrige Rose* | *Rosier à feuilles rougeâtres* ⚬

Rosa moschata. *Rosier musque.*

P. J. Redouté pinx.   Imprimerie de Remond.   Chapuy sculp.

ROSA MOSCHATA HERRM.

Musk Rose | Moschusrose | Rosier musqué ⁘

33

Rosa Bracteata.

Rosier de Macartney.

P.J. Redouté pinx.

Imprimerie de Rémond.

Chapuy sculp.

ROSA BRACTEATA WENDL.

Macartney Rose | Macartney-Rose | Rosier Macartney ⁑

Rosa centifolia Bullata.
Rosier à feuilles de Laitue.

P. J. Redouté pinx.   Imprimerie de Rémond   Langlois sculp.

ROSA CENTIFOLIA L. 'BULLATA'
Lettuce-leaved Cabbage Rose | Salatrose | Rosier à feuilles de Laitue [35]

Rosa muscosa. *Rosier mousseux.*

P.J. Redouté pinx.   Imprimerie de Rémond   Gouten sculp.

ROSA CENTIFOLIA L. 'ANDREWSII'

Single Moss Rose 'Andrewsii' | Einfache Moosrose 'Andrewsii' | Rosier Mousseux à fleurs simples 'Andrewsii'

Rosa muscosa multiplex. *Rosier mousseux à fleurs doubles.*

P. J. Redouté pinx.　　　Imprimerie de Rémond　　　Langlois sculp.

ROSA CENTIFOLIA L. 'MUSCOSA'

Double Moss Rose | Gefüllte Moosrose | Rosier mousseux à fleurs doubles [37]

Rosa Clynophylla.　　*Rosier à feuilles penchées.*

P. J. Redouté pinx.　　Imprimerie de Rémond　　Chapuy sculp.

ROSA CLINOPHYLLA THORY

Droopy-leaved Rose | Panaschiertblättrige Wildrose | Rosier à feuilles penchées

Rosa Lucida.   *Rosier Luisant.*

P.J. Redouté pinx.   Imprimerie de Rémond   Bessin sculp.

ROSA VIRGINIANA HERRM.

Virginia Rose | Glanzrose | Rosier à feuilles luisantes ⁘

Rosa Kamtschatica.   *Rosier du Kamtschatka.*

P.J. Redouté pinx.   Imprimerie de Rémond   Chapuy sculp.

ROSA RUGOSA THUNB.

Japanese Rose | Kartoffelrose | Rosier à feuilles rugueuses ⚬

Rosa Indica.　　　　　*Rosier des Indes.*

P.J.Redouté pinx.　　　　Imprimerie de Remond.　　　　Chapuy sculp.

ROSA CHINENSIS JACQ. VAR. SEMPERFLORENS KOEHNE
Monthly Rose | Monatsrose | Rosier mensuel

Rosa Indica vulgaris.   *Rosier des Indes commun.*

P.J. Redouté pinx.   Imprimerie de Rémond   Bessin sculp.

ROSA CHINENSIS JACQ. 'OLD BLUSH CHINA'

China Rose 'Old Blush China' | Chinarose 'Old Blush China' | Rosier de Chine 'Old Blush China'

Rosa Indica acuminata.   *Rosier des Indes à pétales pointus.*

P. J. Redouté pinx.   Imprimerie de Rémond   Chapuy sculp.

ROSA CHINENSIS JACQ. VAR. MINIMA VOSS

Fairy Rose | *Zwerg-Bengalrose* | *Rosier nain du Bengale* *

ROSA CANINA L. VAR. MONTEZUMAE HUMB. & BONPL.

Montezuma Rose | Montezuma-Rose | Rosier de Montezuma ❖

Rosa Alpina pendulina. *Rosier des Alpes à fruits pendants.*

P.J. Redouté pinx. Imprimerie de Rémond Bessin sculp.

ROSA PENDULINA L. VAR. PENDULINA

Alpine Rose | Alpenheckenrose | Rosier des Alpes ❧

Rosa Alpina Lœvis. Rosier des Alpes à pedoncule et calice glabres.

ROSA BLANDA AITON

Hudson Bay Rose | Eschenrose | Rosier à feuilles de frêne ⁕

Rosa Indica fragrans.   *Rosier des Indes odorant.*
(vulg. Bengale à odeur de thé.)

P.J. Redouté pinx.
Imprimerie de Remond   Langlois sculp.

ROSA × ODORATA SWEET 'HUME'S BLUSH TEA SCENTED CHINA'
Tea Rose 'Hume's Blush Tea scented China' | *Teerose 'Hume's Blush Tea scented China'*
Rosier à odeur de thé 'Hume's Blush Tea scented China'

Rosa Damascena subalba.　　*Rosier de Damas à Petale teinté de rose.*

P.J. Redouté pinx.　　Imprimerie de Remond.　　Chapuy sculp.

ROSA × DUPONTII DÉSÉGL.

Blush Gallica | Dupont-Rose | Rosier de Damas 'Petale teinte de rose' ❖

Rosa Pomponia.   *Rosier Pompon.*

P. J. Redouté pinx.   Imprimerie de Rémond   Langlois sculp.

ROSA CENTIFOLIA L. 'DE MEAUX'

Moss Rose 'De Meaux' | Dijon-Rose | Rosier Pompon 'De Meaux'[sea]

Rosa Villosa, Pomifera.　　*Rosier Velu, Pomifère.*

P.J. Redouté pinx.　　Imprimerie de Rémond.　　Chapuy sculp.

ROSA VILLOSA L.

Apple Rose | Apfelrose | Rosier pomme ❧

Rosa Eglanteria.   *Rosier Eglantier.*

P.J. Redouté pinx.   Imprimerie de Rémond.   Langlois sculp.

ROSA FOETIDA HERRM.

Austrian Yellow Rose | Fuchsrose | Rosier fétide

Rosa Eglanteria var. punicea.   *Rosier Eglantier var. couleur ponceau.*

P.J. Redouté pinx.   Imprimerie de Rémond   Coutan sculp.

ROSA FOETIDA HERRM. 'BICOLOR'
Austrian Copper Rose | Kapuzinerrose | Rosier Capucine [84]

Rosa Gallica officinalis.　　　　*Rosier de Provins ordinaire.*

P.J. Redouté pinx.　　　Imprimerie de Rémond　　　Langlois sculp.

ROSA GALLICA L. 'OFFICINALIS'

Apothecary's Rose | Apothekerrose | Rosier des Apothicaires

Rosa Centifolia simplex. *Rosier Centfeuilles à fleurs simples.*

P. J. Redouté pinx. Imprimerie de Remond Chapuy sculp.

ROSA CENTIFOLIA L. 'SIMPLEX'

Single Cabbage Rose | Einfache Zentifolie | Rosier à centfeuilles à fleurs simples

Rosa Centifolia carnea.

Rosier Vilmorin.

P. J. Redouté pinx.

Imprimerie de Rémond.

Charlin sculp.

ROSA CENTIFOLIA L. CV.

Variety of Cabbage Rose | Zentifolien-Sorte | Variété du Rosier à centfeuilles ᵉᵗ

Rosa Carolina Corymbosa.

Rosier de Caroline en Corymbe.

P. J. Redouté *pinx.*

Imprimerie de Remond

Langlois sculp.

ROSA CAROLINA L.

Pasture Rose | Wiesenrose | Rosier des prés ⁕

Rosa Pimpinelli folia Mariæburgensis. *Rosier de Marienbourg.*

P.J. Redouté pinx. Imprimerie de Remond. Chapuy sculp.

ROSA PIMPINELLIFOLIA L. CV.

Burnet Rose of Marienburg | Bibernellrose 'Marienburg' | Rosier Pimprenelle de Marienbourg

Rosa Pimpinelli folia Pumila.　　*Petit Rosier Pimprenelle.*

P. J. Redouté pinx.　　Imprimerie de Rémond　　Chapuy sculp.

ROSA PIMPINELLIFOLIA L. VAR. PIMPINELLIFOLIA

Burnet Rose | *Bibernellrose* | *Rosier Pimprenelle* ❈

Rosa Muscosa alba   *Rosier Mousseux à fleurs blanches.*

P.J. Redouté pinx.   Imprimerie de Rémond.   Langlois sculp.

ROSA CENTIFOLIA L. VAR. MUSCOSA 'ALBA'

White Moss Rose | Weiße Moosrosen-Sorte | *Rosier mousseux à fleurs blanches* ^{bis}

Rosa arvensis ovata.　　　*Rosier des champs à fruits ovoïdes.*

P. J. Redouté pinx.　　　Imprimerie de Rémond.　　　Chapuy sculp.

ROSA ARVENSIS HUDSON

Field Rose | Feldrose | Eglantier des Champs ✤

Rosa Brevistyla leucochroa.

Rosier à court-style
(var. à fleurs jaunes et blanches).

P.J. Redouté pinx.   Imprimerie de Rémond   Lemaire sculp.

ROSA STYLOSA DESV. VAR. SYSTYLA
— | Griffelrosen-Sorte | Rosier à court-style (var. à fleurs jaunes et blanches) *

Rosa Rubiginosa triflora. *Rosier Rouillé à trois fleurs.*

P.J. Redouté pinx. Imprimerie de Rémond. Chapuy sculp.

? *ROSA RUBIGINOSA* L. VAR. *UMBELLATA*

Variety of Sweet Briar | Weinrosen-Sorte | Variété du Rosier rubigineux ⁕

Rosa Hudsoniana Salicifolia.   *Rosier d'Hudson à feuilles de Saule.*

P. J. Redouté pinx.   Imprimerie de Rémond   Langlois sculp.

ROSA PALUSTRIS MARSHALL

Marsh Rose | Sumpfrose | Rosier des Marais ✿

Rosa alba Regalis   *Rosier blanc Royal.*

P. J. Redouté pinx.   Imprimerie de Rémond.   Bessin sculp.

ROSA × ALBA L. 'GREAT MAIDEN'S BLUSH'

White Rose 'Great Maiden's Blush' | Weiße Rose 'Great Maiden's Blush' | Rosier blanc 'Great Maiden's Blush' [64]

Rosa Moschata flore semi-pleno.

Rosier Muscade à fleurs semi-doubles.

P. J. Redouté *pinx.*

Imprimerie de Rémond

Charlin sculp.

ROSA MOSCHATA HERRM. ʻSEMIPLENAʼ

Semi-double Musk Rose | Halbgefüllte Moschusrose | Rosier musqué à fleurs semi-doubles [65]

Rosa Redutea glauca. *Rosier Redouté à feuilles glauques.*

P.J. Redouté pinx. Imprimerie de Rémond. Chapuy sculp.

ROSA GLAUCA POURRET × ? ROSA PIMPINELLIFOLIA L.

Redouté Rose | Redouté-Rose | Rosier Redouté [**]

Rosa Redutea rubescens. *Rosier Redouté à tiges et à épines rouges.*

P. J. Redouté pinx.   Imprimerie de Rémond   Bessin sculp.

ROSA VILLOSA L. × ROSA PIMPINELLIFOLIA L.

Redouté Rose with red stems and prickles | Rotstielige Redouté-Rose | Rosier Redouté à tiges et à épines rouges

Rosa Cinnamomea Maialis.   *Rosier de Mai.*

P. J. Redouté pinx.   Imprimerie de Rémond.   Chapuy sculp.

ROSA MAJALIS HERRM. 'FOECUNDISSIMA'
Double May Rose | Gefüllte Mairose | Rosier de Mai à fleurs doubles *

Rosa bifera officinalis.   *Rosier des Parfumeurs.*

P.J. Redouté pinx.   Imprimerie de Rémond   Langlois sculp.

ROSA × BIFERA PERS.

Autumn Damask Rose | Herbst-Damaszenerrose | Rosier damascène d'Automne

Rosa Damascena Coccinea　　　*Rosier de Portland.*

P.J. Redouté pinx.　　　Imprimerie de Rémond　　　Bessin sculp.

ROSA HYBRIDA 'DUCHESS OF PORTLAND'

Portland Rose 'Duchess of Portland' | Portland-Rose 'Duchess of Portland' | Rosier de Portland 'Duchess of Portland'

Rosa Centifolia mutabilis.　　　　　*Rosier unique.*

P.J. Redouté pinx.　　　Imprimerie de Rémond.　　　Bessin sculp.

ROSA CENTIFOLIA L. 'UNIQUE BLANCHE'

Cabbage Rose 'White Provence' | Zentifolie 'Unique blanche' | Rosier à centfeuilles 'Unique blanche'

Rosa Centifolia Caryophyllea.   *Rosier Œillet.*

P. J. Redouté pinx.   Imprimerie de Rémond   Charlin sculp.

ROSA CENTIFOLIA L. CV.

Carnation petalled variety of Cabbage Rose | Nelkenblütige Zentifolien-Sorte | Rosier œillet [ct]

Rosa Indica Pumila.   *Rosier nain du Bengale.*

P. J. Redouté *pinx*   *Imprimerie de Rémond*   Chapuy *sculp.*

ROSA CHINENSIS JACQ. VAR. MINIMA VOSS

Double Miniature Rose | Gefüllte Zwerg-Bengalrose | Rosier nain du Bengale pompon

Rosa alba flore pleno.

Rosier blanc ordinaire.

P. J. Redouté pinx.

Imprimerie de Rémond

Langlois sculp.

ROSA × ALBA L. 'SEMIPLENA'

Semi-double White Rose | Halbgefüllte Weiße Rose | Rosier blanc ordinaire

Rosa Pimpinellifolia rubra.
(*Flore multiplici.*)

Rosier Pimprenelle rouge.
(*Variété à fleurs doubles.*)

P.J. Redouté pinx.   Imprimerie de Remond   Chapuy sculp.

ROSA PIMPINELLIFOLIA L. 'DOUBLE PINK SCOTCH BRIAR'
Burnet Rose 'Double Pink Scotch Briar' | Bibernellrose 'Double Pink Scotch Briar'
Rosier Pimprenelle 'Double Pink Scotch Briar'

Rosa Bifera alba. *Rosier des quatre Saisons à fleurs blanches.*

P.J. Redouté pinx. Imprimerie de Rémond. Bessin sculp.

ROSA × BIFERA PERS.

White variety of Autumn Damask Rose | Weiße Herbst-Damaszenerrose | Variété du Rosier damascène d'Automne à fleurs blanches [et]

Rosa Indica Cruenta.

Rosier du Bengale à fleurs pourpre de sang.

P. J. Redouté pinx.   Imprimerie de Remond   Langlois sculp.

ROSA CHINENSIS JACQ. VAR. *SEMPERFLORENS* KOEHNE 'SLATER'S CRIMSON CHINA'

Monthly Rose 'Slater's Crimson China' | Monatsrose 'Slater's Crimson China' | Rosier mensuel 'Slater's Crimson China' [76]

Rosa Rubiginosa Cretica. *Rosier de Crête.*

P. J. Redouté pinx. Imprimerie de Remond. Langlois sculp.

ROSA RUBIGINOSA L.

Sweet Briar | Weinrose | Rosier rubigineux ❧

Rosa Turbinata. *Rosier de Francfort.*

P.J. Redouté pinx. Imprimerie de Remond Bessin sculp.

ROSA 'FRANCOFURTANA'

'Empress Josephine' | 'Impératrice Joséphine' | 'Impératrice Joséphine'

Rosa Leucantha.   *Rosier à fleurs blanches.*

P. J. Redouté pinx   Imprimerie de Remond.   Langlois sculp.

? *ROSA DUMETORUM* THUILL. 'OBTUSIFOLIA'
— | Flaumrose 'Obtusifolia' | Rosier à fleurs blanches ❧

Rosa fœtida.

Rosier à fruit fétide.

P. J. Redouté pinx.

Imprimerie de Remond

Chapuy sculp.

? *ROSA TOMENTOSA* SMITH VAR. *BRITANNICA*

Foul-fruited varitey of Tomentose Rose | Filzrosen-Sorte | Variété du Rosier Tomenteux

Rosa Cinnamomea flore simplici.   *Rosier de Mai à fleurs simples.*

P. J. Redouté pinx.   Imprimerie de Rémond.   Charlin sculp.

ROSA MAJALIS HERRM.

May Rose | *Mairose* | *Rosier de Mai* ❖

Rosa Gallica Versicolor.   *Rosier de France à fleurs panachées.*

P. J. Redouté pinx.   *Imprimerie de Remond*   *Langlois sculp.*

ROSA GALLICA L. 'VERSICOLOR'

French Rose 'Versicolor' | Panaschiert blühende Essigrose | Rosier de France à fleurs panachées [85]

Rosa Damascena Variegata.

Rosier d'Yorck et de Lancastre.

P. J. Redouté pinx.

Imprimerie de Remond

Bessin sculp.

ROSA × DAMASCENA MILLER 'VERSICOLOR'

Damask Rose 'York and Lancaster' | Damaszenerrose 'York and Lancaster' | Rosier d'Yorck et de Lancastre [86]

Rosa Rubiginosa Zabeth.   *Eglantine de la Reine Elisabeth.*

P. J. Redouté pinx.   Imprimerie de Rémond   Langlois sculp.

ROSA RUBIGINOSA L. 'ZABETH'

Sweet Briar 'Zabeth' | Weinrose 'Zabeth' | Rosier rubigineux 'Reine Elisabeth' [st]

Rosa Rapa.

Rosier Turneps.

P. J. Redouté pinx.   Imprimerie de Remond   Charlin sculp.

? ROSA × RAPA BOSC

? 'Rose d'Amour' | ? 'Rose d'Amour' | ? Rosier d'Amour

Rosa Andegavensis.   *Rosier d'Anjou.*

P. J. Redouté pinx.   Imprimerie de Remond.   Chapuy sculp.

ROSA CANINA L. VAR. ANDEGAVENSIS BAST.

Anjou Rose | Anjou-Rose | Rosier d'Anjou [85]

Rosa Centifolia Bipinnata.   *Rosier à feuilles de Céleri.*

P.J. Redouté pinx.   Imprimerie de Remond.   Langlois sculp.

ROSA CENTIFOLIA L. CV.
Celery-leaved variety of Cabbage Rose | Sellerieblättrige Zentifolien-Sorte |
Variété du Rosier à centfeuilles à feuilles de Céleri

Rosa Collina fastigiata.   *Rosier Nivelle.*

P. J. Redouté pinx.   Imprimerie de Rémond   Chapuy sculp.

? *ROSA STYLOSA VAR . SYSTYLA FOR . FASTIGIATA*
— | *Griffelrose* | *Rosier des Collines* ❖

Rosa Semper-Virens globosa.   *Rosier grimpant à fruits globuleux.*

P. J. Redouté pinx.   Imprimerie de Remond   Chapuy sculp.

ROSA SEMPERVIRENS L.

Evergreen Rose | Immergrüne Rose | Rosier à feuilles persistantes ❧

Rosa Gallica Purpurea Velutina, Parva. *Rosier de Van-Eeden.*

P.J. Redouté pinx.   *Imprimerie de Rémond*   *Langlois sculp.*

ROSA GALLICA L. CV. ? 'TUSCANY'

Variety of French Rose ? 'Tuscany'? | Essigrosen-Sorte ? 'Tuscany'? | Variété du Rosier de France *

Rosa Gallica Regalis.　　　　　*Rosier Grandeur Royale.*

P.J. Redouté pinx.　　　　Imprimerie de Rémond　　　　Bessin sculp.

ROSA GALLICA L. HYBR.

Provins royal | Essigrosen-Hybride | Rosier de France var. Grandeur Royale &

Rosa Orbessanea.   *Rosier d'Orbessan.*

P.J. Redouté pinx.   Imprimerie de Rémond.   Lemaire sculp.

ROSA × FRANCOFURTANA THORY

? 'Francofurtana' | ? Frankfurter Rose | ? Rosier d'Orbessan

Rosa Rubiginosa nemoralis.   *L'Eglantine des bois.*

P.J. Redouté pinx.   Imprimerie de Rémond   Chapuy sculp.

ROSA MICRANTHA BORRER VAR. MICRANTHA

Small flowered Eglantine | *Kleinblütige Rose* | *Eglantier des bois* ❖

Rosa Indica Pumila,
(flore simplici).

Petit Rosier du Bengale,
(à fleurs simples).

P.J. Redouté pinx.   Imprimerie de Remond   Chapuy sculp.

ROSA CHINENSIS JACQ. VAR. MINIMA VOSS CV.

Variety of Fairy Rose | Zwerg-Bengalrosen-Sorte | Rosier nain du Bengale à fleurs simples

ROSA CHINENSIS JACQ. VAR. LONGIFOLIA REHDER

China Rose 'Longifolia' | Chinarose 'Longifolia' | Rosier de Chine à feuilles de Pêcher

Rosa Gallica.   *Rosier Evêque.*
(*Purpuro-violacea magna.*)

P. J. Redouté pinx.   Imprimerie de Remond.   Langlois sculp.

ROSA GALLICA L. 'THE BISHOP'

French Rose 'The Bishop' | Essigrose 'The Bishop' | Rosier Evêque

Rosa aciphylla.　　　　　　　　*Rosier cuspidé.*

P. J. Redouté pinx.　　　　　Imprimerie de Rémond.　　　　　Chapuy sculp.

ROSA CANINA L. VAR. *LUTETIANA* BAKER FOR. *ACIPHYLLA*
Needle-leaved Dog Rose | Nadelblättrige Hundsrose | Variété du Rosier de Chien

Rosa Malmundariensis.　　　　*Rosier de Malmedy.*

P. J. Redouté *pinx.*　　　　*Imprimerie de Rémond.*　　　　*Langlois sculp.*

ROSA DUMALIS BECHSTEIN VAR. MALMUNDARIENSIS

Malmedy Rose | *Malmedy-Rose* | *Rosier de Malmedy* ✣

Rosa Indica. *Rosier du Bengale (Cent feuille).*

P. J. Redouté pinx. Imprimerie de Remond Charlin sculp.

ROSA CHINENSIS JACQ. VAR. MINIMA VOSS

China Rose | Bengalrose | La Bengale bichonne

Rosa Indica.　　　*La Bengale bichonne.*

P. J. Redouté pinx.　　　Imprimerie de Rémond　　　Langlois sculp.

ROSA CHINENSIS JACQ. 'MULTIPETALA'

Double variety of China Rose | Gefüllte Chinarosen-Sorte | Rosier de Chine à fleurs doubles [105]

Rosa Tomentosa.   *Rosier Cotonneux.*

P.J. Redouté pinx.   Imprimerie de Rémond.   Langlois sculp.

ROSA TOMENTOSA SMITH

Tomentose Rose | Filzrose | Rosier Tomenteux ✤

Rosa Damascena aurora. *Rosier Aurore Poniatowska.*

P. J. Redouté pinx.   Imprimerie de Remond.   Chardin sculp.

ROSA × ALBA L. 'CELESTE'

White Rose 'Celestial' | Weiße Rose 'Celeste' | Rosier blanc 'Celeste' [96]

Rosa Banksiæ. *Rosier de Lady Banks.*

P. J. Redouté pinx. Imprimerie de Rémond Chapuy sculp.

ROSA BANKSIAE AITON FIL. VAR. BANKSIAE 'ALBA PLENA'

Banks Rose 'Lady Banksia Snowflake' | *Weiße, gefüllte Banksrose* | *Rosier de Lady Banks à fleurs blanches et doubles* [16]

Rosa Candolleana Elegans. *Rosier de Candolle.*

P. J. Redouté pinx. Imprimerie de Remond. Langlois sculp.

ROSA × REVERSA WALDST. & KIT.

De Candolle Rose | De Candolle-Rose | Rosier de Candolle ❖

Rosa Alba Cimbæfolia.   *Rosier blanc à feuilles de Chanvre.*

P.J. Redouté pinx.   Imprimerie de Rémond.   Bessin sculp.

ROSA × ALBA L. 'À FEUILLES DE CHANVRE'

White Rose 'À feuilles de Chanvre' | Weiße Rose 'À feuilles de Chanvre' | Rosier blanc 'À feuilles de Chanvre'

Rosa Sempervirens latifolia.   *Rosier grimpant à grandes feuilles.*

P.J. Redouté pinx.   Imprimerie de Rémond.   Langlois sculp.

ROSA SEMPERVIRENS L. CV.

Variety of Evergreen Rose | Sorte der Immergrünen Rose | Variété du Rosier à feuilles persistantes

ROSA CANINA L. VAR. LUTETIANA BAKER
Variety of Dog Rose | *Hundsrosen-Sorte* | *Variété du Rosier de Chien*

Rosa Damascena.

Rosier de Cels.

P. J. Redouté pinx.

Imprimerie de Rémond

Charlin sculp.

ROSA × DAMASCENA MILLER 'CELSIANA'

Damask Rose 'Celsiana' | Damaszenerrose 'Celsiana' | Rosier damascène 'Celesiana'

Rosa Alpina flore variegato.   *Rosier des Alpes à fleurs panachées.*

P. J. Redouté *pinx.*   Imprimerie de Remond.   Chapuy *sculp.*

ROSA BLANDA AITON CV.

Striped variety of Hudson Bay Rose | *Gestreifte Eschenrosen-Sorte* | *Rosier de frêne à fleurs panachées*

Rosa Pomponia flore subsimplici.   *Rosier* Pompon à fleurs presque simples.

P. J. Redouté pinx.   Imprimerie de Remond   Chapuy Sculp.

ROSA CENTIFOLIA L. CV.

Variety of Cabbage Rose | *Zentifolien-Sorte* | *Variété du Rosier à centfeuilles*

Rosa centifolia foliacea.   *Rosier à cent feuilles, foliacé.*

P. J. Redouté *pinx.*   *Imprimerie de Rémond*   *Langlois Sculp.*

ROSA CENTIFOLIA L. CV.

Variety of Cabbage Rose | Zentifolien-Sorte | Variété du Rosier à centfeuilles [et]

Rosa sepium rosea.   *Rosier des hayes à fleurs roses.*

P. J. Redouté pinx.   Imprimerie de Remond.   Lemaire sculp.

ROSA AGRESTIS SAVI VAR. SEPIUM THUILL.

Grassland Rose | *Ackerrosen-Sorte* | *Rosier des hayes* ❧

Rosa Pumila.

Rosier d'Amour.

P. J. Redouté pinx .

Imprimerie de Rémond

Bessin sculp.

ROSA GALLICA L. VAR. PUMILA

Creeping French Rose | Kriechende Essigrose | Rosier d'Amour ❖

Rosa Centifolia crenata. *Rosier Centfeuilles à folioles crenelées.*

P. J. Redouté pinx. Imprimerie de Rémond Chapuy sculp.

ROSA CENTIFOLIA L. CV.

Variety of Cabbage Rose | Zentifolien-Sorte | Variété du Rosier à centfeuilles

Rosa Multiflora carnea.　　　　　*Rosier Multiflore a fleurs carnées.*

ROSA MULTIFLORA THUNB. VAR. MULTIFLORA

Pink double Multiflora | Rosa, gefüllte Vielblütige Rose | Rosier du Japon à fleurs carnées

Rosa Multiflora platyphylla.   *Rosier Multiflore à grandes feuilles.*

P.J. Redouté pinx.   Imprimerie de Rémond   Langlois sculp.

ROSA MULTIFLORA THUNB. VAR. PLATYPHYLLA REHDER ET WILSON 'SEVEN SISTERS ROSE'

Multiflora 'Seven Sisters Rose' | Vielblütige Rose 'Seven Sisters Rose' | Rosier du Japon 'Seven Sisters Rose' [115]

Rosa Villosa Terebenthina.　　　　*Rosier Velu à odeur de Térébenthine*

P.J. Redouté pinx.　　　Imprimerie de Remond.　　　Bessin sculp.

ROSA L. HORT

Rosa parvi-flora.　　　　*Rosier à petites fleurs.*

P. J. Redouté pinx.　　　Imprimerie de Rémond.　　　Langlois sculp.

ROSA CAROLINA L. 'PLENA'

Double Pasture Rose | Gefüllte Wiesenrosen-Sorte | Rosier des prés à fleurs doubles

Rosa Rubiginosa flore semi-pleno.   *Rosier Rouillé à fleurs semi-doubles.*

P. J. Redouté pinx. Imprimerie de Remond. Chapuy sculp.

ROSA RUBIGINOSA L. 'SEMIPLENA'

Semi-double Sweet Briar | Halbgefüllte Weinrose | Rosier rubigineux à fleurs semi-doubles

Rosa *Noisettiana.*

Rosier *de Philippe Noisette.*

P. J. Redouté *pinx.*

Imprimerie de Rémond

Langlois sculp.

? ROSA × NOISETTIANA THORY

? *Noisette Rose* | ? *Noisette-Rose* | ? *Rosier de Noisette*

Rosa Indica subalba.

Rosier du Bengale à fleurs blanches.

P.J. Redouté pinx.

Imprimerie de Remond.

Lemaire sculp.

ROSA CHINENSIS JACQ. VAR. SEMPERFLORENS KOEHNE CV.

Variety of Monthly Rose | Monatsrosen-Sorte | Varieté du Rosier mensuel [et]

Rosa Nivea.

Rosier blanc de Neige.

P. J. Redouté pinx.   Imprimerie de Remond   Langlois sculp.

ROSA LAEVIGATA MICHAUX

Cherokee Rose | Cherokee-Rose | Cherokee Rose [US]

Rosa geminata.   *Rosier à fleurs géminées.*

P. J. Redouté pinx.   Imprimerie de Remond   Chapuy sculp.

ROSA × POLLINIANA SPRENGEL [91A]

Rosa Dumetorum. *Rosier des Buissons.*

P.J. Redouté pinx. Imprimerie de Remond. Chapuy sculp.

ROSA CORYMBIFERA BORKH.

— | Buschrose | Rosier des Buissons ✣

Rosa Tomentosa.   *Rosier Cotonneux.*

P. J. Redouté pinx.   Imprimerie de Rémond.   Bessin sculp.

ROSA TOMENTOSA SMITH CV.

Double variety of Tomentose Rose | Gefüllte Filzrosen-Sorte | Variété du Rosier Tomenteux à fleurs doubles

Rosa mollissima.

Rosier à feuilles molles.

P. J. Redouté pinx.   Imprimerie de Remond.   Victor sculp.

ROSA TOMENTOSA SMITH CV.

Semi-double variety of Tomentose Rose | Halbgefüllte Filzrosen-Sorte | Variété du Rosier Tomenteux à fleurs semi-doubles

Rosa Gallica caerulea.   *Rosier de Provins à feuilles bleuâtres.*

P.J. Redouté pinx.   Imprimerie de Remond.   Eug. Talbaux sculp.

ROSA GALLICA L. CV.

Variety of French Rose | Essigrosen-Sorte | Variété du Rosier de France

Rosa Inermis.

Rosier Turbiné sans épines.

P.J. Redouté pinx.

Imprimerie de Remond

Lemaire sculp.

ROSA × L'HERITIERANEA THORY CV.

Boursault Rose | Boursault-Rose | Rosier de Boursault

Rosa Campanulata alba.   *Rosier Campanulé à fleurs blanches.*

P. J. Redouté pinx.   Imprimerie de Rémond   Langlois sculp.

Rosa rubiginosa aculeatissima.   *Rosier rouillé très épineux.*

P. J. Redouté pinx.   Imprimerie de Remond.   Chapuy Sculp.

ROSA RUBIGINOSA L. VAR. UMBELLATA

Variety of Sweet Briar | *Weinrosen-Sorte* | *Rosier rubigineux très épineux* [?]

Rosa Pimpinellifolia alba
flore multiplei.

Rosier Pimprenelle blanc
à fleurs doubles.

P. J. Redouté pinx.

Imprimerie de Rémond

Teillard sculp.

ROSA PIMPINELLIFOLIA L. CV.
Semi-double variety of Burnet Rose | Halbgefüllte Bibernellrosen-Sorte | Variété du Rosier Pimprenelle à fleurs semi-doubles

Rosa centifolia Anglica rubra. *Rosier de Cumberland.*

P. J. Redouté pinx. Imprimerie de Remond. Langlois sculp.

ROSA CENTIFOLIA L. CV.

Variety of Cabbage Rose | Zentifolien-Sorte | Variété du Rosier à centfeuilles

Rosa Pimpinellifolia flore variegato.   La Pimprenelle aux Cent-Ecus.

P. J. Redouté pinx.   Imprimerie de Remond.   Langlois Sculp.

ROSA PIMPINELLIFOLIA L. VAR. CIPHIANA

Variegated flowering variety of Burnet Rose | Panaschiertblütige Bibernellrosen-Sorte

Variété du Rosier Pimprenelle à fleurs panachées

Rosa Gallica Granatus.　　　*Rosier de France à Pomme de Grenade.*

P.J. Redouté pinx.　　　Imprimerie de Rémond　　　Victor sculp.

ROSA GALLICA L. CV.

Variety of French Rose | Essigrosen-Sorte | Variété du Rosier de France

Rosa sepium flore submultiplici.   *Rosier des hayes à fleurs semi doubles.*

P. J. Redouté pinx.   Imprimerie de Remond.   Eug. Talbeaux sculp.

ROSA AGRESTIS SAVI CV.

Semi-double variety of Grassland Rose | Halbgefüllte Ackerrosen-Sorte | Rosier des hayes à fleurs semi-doubles &

Rosa Hudsoniana scandens. *Rosier d'Hudson à tiges grimpantes.*

P. J. Redouté pinx. Imprimerie de Remond. Tilliard sculp.

? *ROSA PALUSTRIS* MARSHALL CV.

Semi-double variety of Marsh Rose | Halbgefüllte Sumpfrosen-Sorte | Variété du Rosier d'Hudson à fleurs semi-doubles

Rosa Alpina vulgaris.

Rosier des Alpes commun.

P. J. Redouté pinx.

Imprimerie de Rémond.

Chapuy sculp.

ROSA PENDULINA L. VAR. PENDULINA

Alpine Rose | Alpenheckenrose | Rosier des Alpes ⁕

Rosa Rosenbergiana.

Rosier de Rosenberg.

P. J. Redouté pinx.

Imprimerie de Rémond.

Langlois sculp.

? ROSA × RAPA BOSC CV.

— | Gefüllte Glanzrose | Rosier de Rosenberg

Rosa Centifolia Anemonoides.   *La Centfeuilles Anemone.*

P. J. Redouté pinx.   Imprimerie de Rémond   Victor sculp.

ROSA CENTIFOLIA L. 'ANEMONOIDES'

Cabbage Rose 'Anemonoides' | Anemonenblütige Zentifolie | Rosier à centfeuilles à fleurs d'anémone

Rosa hudsoniana Subcorymbosa. *Rosier d'Hudson à fleurs presqu'en Corymbe.*

P.J. Redouté pinx.   Imprimerie de Remond.   Eug. Talbaur sculp.

ROSA PALUSTRIS MARSHALL CV.
Semi-double variety of Marsh Rose | Halbgefüllte Sumpfrosen-Sorte
Variété du Rosier d'Hudson à fleurs semi-doubles

Rosa Indica subviolacea.   *Rosier des Indes à fleurs presque violettes.*

P. J. Redouté pinx.   Imprimerie de Remond   Langlois sculp.

ROSA CHINENSIS JACQ. VAR. SEMPERFLORENS KOEHNE

Monthly Rose | *Monatsrose* | *Rosier mensuel* ^{et}

Rosa Gallica Pontiana.　　　　*Rosier du Pont.*

P. J. Redouté pinx.　　　　Imprimerie de Rémond　　　　Bessin sculp.

ROSA GALLICA L. CV.

Variety of French Rose | Essigrosen-Sorte | Variété du Rosier de France

Rosa Gallica latifolia. Rosier de Provins à grandes feuilles.

P. J. Redouté pinx. Imprimerie de Remond Langlois sculp.

ROSA GALLICA L. × ? ROSA CENTIFOLIA L.

Large-leaved variety of French Rose | Großblättrige Essigrosen-Sorte | Variété du Rosier de France à grandes feuilles

Rosa Spinulifolia Dematratiana. *Rosier Spinulé de Dematra.*

P.J. Redouté pinx. Imprimerie de Rémond Chapuy sculp.

ROSA × SPINULIFOLIA DEMATRA

Wild hybrid of Alpine Rose | Naturhybride der Alpenrose | Rosier des Alpes — hybride spontané ❖

Rosa Bifera macrocarpa.   *La Quatre Saisons Lelieur.*

ROSA × DAMASCENA MILLER × ROSA CHINENSIS JACQ. VAR. SEMPERFLORENS KOEHNE 'ROSE DU ROI'
Portland Rose 'Rose du Roi' | Portlandrose 'Rose du Roi' | Rosier de Portland 'Rose du Roi' [sic]

Rosa Myriacantha.   *Rosier à Mille-Épines.*

P. J. Redouté pinx.   Imprimerie de Rémond.   Chapuy sculp.

? ROSA PIMPINELLIFOLIA L. VAR. MYRIACANTHA SER.
Prickly variety of Burnet Rose | Stachelige Bibernellrosen-Sorte | Variété du Rosier Pimprenelle à mille épines ❖

ROSA × DAMASCENA MILLER 'CELSIANA'

Damask Rose 'Celsiana' | *Damaszenerrose 'Celsiana'* | *Rosier damascène 'Celsiana'*

Rosa Alpina debilis.

Rosier des Alpes à tiges foibles.

P.J. Redouté pinx.

Imprimerie de Remond

Bessin sculp.

? *ROSA* × *REVERSA* WALDST. & KIT.

Wild hybrid of Alpine Rose | Naturhybride der Alpenheckenrose | Rosier des Alpes — hybride spontané ❖

Rosa alba foliacea.   *La Blanche foliacée de fleury.*

P. J. Redouté pinx.   Imprimerie de Rémond   Victor sculp.

ROSA × ALBA L. CV.

Variety of White Rose with pinnate sepals | Weiße Rosen-Sorte mit gefiederten Sepalen | Variété du Rosier blanc

Rosa Eglanteria Luteola.

L'Eglantier Serin.

P. J. Redouté pinx.

Imprimerie de Rémond.

Langlois sculp.

ROSA × HARISONII RIVERS 'LUTEA'

'Yellow Rose of Texas' | 'Yellow Rose of Texas' | Eglantier Serin ™

Rosa l'heritieranea.   *Rosier l'héritier.*

P. J. Redouté pinx.   Imprimerie de Remond.   Victor sculp.

ROSA × L'HERITIERANEA THORY

Boursault Rose | Boursault-Rose | Rosier de Boursault

Rosa Pimpinelli-folia inermis. *Rosier Pimprenelle à tiges sans épines.*

P. J. Redouté pinx. Imprimerie de Remond. Langlois sculp.

? *ROSA PIMPINELLIFOLIA* L. VAR. *INERMIS* DC.

Thornless Burnet Rose | Stachellose Bibernellrose | Rosier Pimprenelle à tiges sans épines ❖

Rosa Rubiginosa anemone-flora. *Rosier Rouillé à fleurs d'anémone.*

 Imprimerie de Rémond. *Langlois sculp.*

ROSA RUBIGINOSA L. CV.

Variety of Sweet Briar | *Anemonenblütige Weinrosen-Sorte* | *Rosier rubigineux à fleurs d'anémone* ⚹

Rosa Biserrata. *Rosier des Montagnes à folioles bidentées.*

P. J. Redouté pinx. Imprimerie de Remond. Chapuy Sculp.

ROSA DUMALIS BECHSTEIN VAR. MALMUNDARIENSIS FOR BISERRATA

? Double serrated Malmedy-Rose | ? Doppeltgesägte Malmedy-Rose | ? Rosier de Malmedy à folioles bidentées ✢

Rosa Gallica Aurelianensis   *La Duchesse d'Orléans.*

P. J. Redouté pinx.   Imprimerie de Remond   Langlois sculp.

ROSA GALLICA L. CV. ? 'DUCHESSE D'ORLÉANS'

French Rose ? 'Duchesse d'Orléans' | Essigrose ? 'Duchesse d'Orléans' | Rosier de France ? 'Duchesse d'Orléans'

Rosa Stylosa.

Rosier des Champs à tiges érigées.

P. J. Redouté pinx.

Imprimerie de Rémond

Chapuy sculp.

ROSA STYLOSA DESV. VAR. STYLOSA
— | Griffelrose | Rosier à court-style ❖

Rosa Centifolia Burgundiaca. *La Cent-feuilles de Bordeaux.*

P. J. Redouté pinx.   Imprimerie de Rémond.   Langlois sculp.

ROSA CENTIFOLIA L. 'PETITE DE HOLLANDE'

Cabbage Rose 'Petite de Hollande' | Zentifolie 'Petite de Hollande'

Rosier à centfeuilles 'Petite de Hollande'

Rosa Gallica agatha. (Varietas parva violacea.)   *La petite Renoncule violette.*

P. J. Redouté pinx.   Imprimerie de Rémond   Lemaire sculp.

ROSA GALLICA L. CV. / ROSA CENTIFOLIA L. CV.
Variety of French Rose or Cabbage Rose | Essigrosen- oder Zentifolien-Sorte
Variété du Rosier de France ou du Rosier à centfeuilles

Rosa Damascena Italica.   *La Quatre-Saisons d'Italie.*

P.J.Redouté pinx.   Imprimerie de Remond   Victor sculp.

ROSA × DAMASCENA MILLER CV.

Variety of Damask Rose | Damaszenerrosen-Sorte | Variété du Rosier damascène

Rosa Gallica agatha (var. Delphiniana). L'Enfant de France.

P.J. Redouté pinx.   Imprimerie de Rémond.   Bessa sculp.

ROSA GALLICA L. CV.

Variety of French Rose | Essigrosen-Sorte | Variété du Rosier de France [et]

Rosa Indica Stelligera.

Le Bengale Etoilé.

P.J.Redouté pinx.

Imprimerie de Remond

Chapuy sculp.

ROSA *CHINENSIS* JACQ. VAR. *SEMPERFLORENS* KOEHNE CV.

Variety of Monthly Rose | *Monatsrosen-Sorte* | *Variété du Rosier mensuel* [d]

Rosa Indica Sertulata.

Le Bengale à Bouquets.

P.J. Redouté pinx.

Imprimerie de Rémond.

Langlois sculp.

ROSA CHINENSIS JACQ. CV.

Variety of China Rose | Chinarosen-Sorte | Variété du Rosier de Chine [a]

Rosa Gallica-Agatha. (Var. Regalis.)   *Rosier Agathe-Royale.*

P.J. Redouté pinx.   Imprimerie de Rémond.   Langlois sculp.

ROSA GALLICA L. — HYBR.

French Rose hybrid | Essigrosen-Hybride | Rosier de France hybride &

Rosa Gallica Agatha. (var. Prolifera.)   *Rosier Agathe Prolifere.*

P.J. Redouté pinx.   Imprimerie de Remond.   Victor sculp.

ROSA GALLICA L. CV.

Variety of French Rose | Essigrosen-Sorte | Variété du Rosier de France

165

Rosa Gallica flore marmoreo.   *Rosier de Provins à fleurs marbrées.*

P. J. Redouté pinx.   Imprimerie de Rémond   Bessin sculp.

ROSA GALLICA L. CV.

Marbled variety of French Rose | Marmoriert blühende Essigrosen-Sorte | Variété du Rosier de France à fleurs marbrées

Rosa Sepium Myrtifolia.   *Rosier des Hayes à feuilles de Myrte.*

P. J. Redouté pinx.   Imprimerie de Rémond   Langlois sculp.

ROSA AGRESTIS SAVI

Grassland Rose | Ackerrose | Rosier des hayes

Rosa Gallica flore giganteo.   *Rosier de Provins à fleur gigantesque.*

P. J. Redouté pinx.   Imprimerie de Remond   Victor sculp.

ROSA GALLICA L. CV.

Large-flowered variety of French Rose | Großblumige Essigrosen-Sorte | Variété du Rosier de France à grandes fleurs

Rosa Gallica Stapeliæ flora.   *Rosier de Provins à fleurs de Stapelie.*

P. J. Redouté pinx.   Imprimerie de Remond   Bessin sculp.

ROSA GALLICA L. CV.

Stapelia-flowered variety of French Rose | Stapelienblütige Essigrosen-Sorte | Variété du Rosier de France à fleurs de Stapelie

Rosa Gallica rosea flore simplici.   *Rosier de Provins à fleurs roses et simples.*

P. J. Redouté pinx.   Imprimerie de Remond   Langlois sculp.

ROSA GALLICA L.

French Rose | Essigrose | Rosier de France

Rosa Bifera pumila. *Le petit Quatre-Saisons.*

P.J. Redouté pinx. Imprimerie de Rémond Lemaire sculp.

ROSA × BIFERA PERS. CV.

Variety of small Autumn Damask Rose | Kleine Herbst-Damaszenerrosen-Sorte | Variété du Petit Quatre Saisons [8]

Rosa farinosa.   *Rosier farineux.*

P.J. Redouté pinx.   Imprimerie de Rémond.   Victor sculp.

ROSA TOMENTOSA SMITH VAR. FARINOSA

Variety of Tomentose Rose | Mehlige Filzrosen-Sorte | Variété du Rosier Tomenteux

Rosa Indica dichotoma.   *Le Bengale animating.*

P.J. Redouté pinx .   Imprimerie de Remond.   Chapuy sculp .

ROSA CHINENSIS JACQ. CV.

Variety of China | Chinarosen-Sorte | Variété du Rosier de Chine

Rosa Centifolia prolifera foliacea.   *La Cent feuilles prolifère foliacée.*

P. J. Redouté *pinx.*   *Imprimerie de Remond*   *Victor sculp.*

ROSA CENTIFOLIA L. CV.

Variety of Cabbage Rose | Zentifolien-Sorte | Variété du Rosier à centfeuilles

Rosa Collina Monsoniana. *Rosier de Ladi-Monson.*

P. J. Redouté pinx. Imprimerie de Rémond. Langlois Sculp.

? *ROSA MONSONIAE* LINDLEY

Rose of Lady Monson | Lady Monson-Rose | Rosier de Lady Monson

Rosa Indica Caryophyllea.   *La Bengale Œillet.*

P.J. Redouté pinx.   Imprimerie de Rémond.   Langlois sculp.

ROSA CHINENSIS JACQ. VAR. SEMPERFLORENS KOEHNE

Monthly Rose | Monatsrose | Rosier mensuel

Rosa Rubifolia.   *Rosier à feuilles de Ronce.*

P. J. Redouté pinx.   Imprimerie de Remond   Victor Sculp.

ROSA SETIGERA MICHAUX

Prairie Rose | Prärierose | Rosier des Prairies ※

Rosa Eglanteria sub rubra. *L'Eglantier Cerise.*

P.J. Redouté pinx. Imprimerie de Rémond Langlois Sculp.

ROSA FOETIDA HERRM. 'BICOLOR'
Austrian Copper Rose | Kapuzinerrose | Rosier Capucine

Rosa Canina grandiflora.　　　*Rosier Canin à grandes fleurs.*

P.J. Redouté pinx.　　　Imprimerie de Remond.　　　Lemaire sculp.

ROSA × WAITZIANA TRATT.

Dog Rose hybrid | Hundsrosen-Hybride | Rosier de Chien hybride ❖

Rosa Gallica Agatha incarnata.　　　　　*L'Agathe Carnée.*

P. J. Redouté pinx.　　　Imprimerie de Rémond　　　Langlois sculp.

ROSA GALLICA L. 'AGATHA INCARNATA'

French Rose Hybrid 'Agatha Incarnata' | *Essigrose 'Agatha Incarnata'* | *Rosier de France 'Agathe Carnée'*

Rosa Gallica Maheka. (flore subsimplici).   *Le Maheka à fleurs simples.*

P. J. Redouté pinx.   Imprimerie de Rémond   Langlois sculp.

ROSA GALLICA L. 'VIOLACEA'

French Rose 'Violacea' | Essigrose 'Violacea' | Rosier de France 'Violacea'

Rosa Reclinata flore simplici.   *Rosier à boutons renversés; Var. à fleurs simples.*

P. J. Redouté pinx.   Imprimerie de Remond   Bessin sculp.

ROSA × L'HERITIERANEA THORY CV.

Single variety of Boursault Rose | Einfache Boursault-Rosensorte | Variété du Rosier de Boursault à fleurs simples [1]

Rosa Reclinata flore sub multiplici.　　　*Rosier à boutons penchés. (var. à fleurs semi doubles.)*

P.J. Redouté pinx.　　　Imprimerie de Remond.　　　Langlois sculp.

ROSA × L'HERITIERANEA THORY

Boursault Rose | Boursault-Rose | Rosier de Boursault

Rosa hispida Argentea.　　　　*Rosier hispide à fleurs Argentées.*

P.J. Redouté pinx.　　　Imprimerie de Rémond　　　Lemaire Sculp.

ROSA VILLOSA L. × ROSA PIMPINELLIFOLIA L.

Apple Rose hybrid | Apfelrosen-Hybride | Rosier pomme hybride

Rosa Ventenatiana.　　　　　*Rosier Ventenat.*

P. J. Redouté pinx.　　　Imprimerie de Rémond　　　Victor sculp.

ROSA PIMPINELLIFOLIA L. — HYBR.

Burnet Rose hybrid | Bibernellrosen-Hybride | Rosier Pimprenelle hybride

Rosa Bifera Variegata. *La Quatre Saisons à feuilles panachées.*

P. J. Redouté *pinx.* Imprimerie de Remond Victor *Sculp.*

ROSA × BIFERA PERS. CV.

Variegated variety of Autumn Damask Rose | Panaschiertblättrige Herbst-Damaszenerrose
Variété du Rosier damascène d'Automne panaché

Rosa sempervirens Leschenaultiana.   *Le Rosier Leschenault.*

P. J. Redouté pinx.   Imprimerie de Remond.   Langlois sculp.

ROSA SEMPERVIRENS L. VAR. LESCHENAULTIANA

Variety of Evergreen Rose | Sorte der Immergrünen Rose | Variété du Rosier à feuilles peristantes

Rosa Gallica Gueriniana. *Rosier Guerin.*

P. J. Redouté pinx. Imprimerie de Rémond Langlois sculp.

? *ROSA GALLICA* L. × *ROSA CHINENSIS* JACQ.

French Rose hybrid | Essigrosen-Hybride | Rosier Guerin

P.J. Redouté pinx.   Imprimerie de Rémond   Langlois sculp.

? ROSA GALLICA L. × ROSA CHINENSIS JACQ.
French Rose hybrid | Essigrosen-Hybride | Rosier Guerin

188

Rosa indica Automnalis. *Le Bengale d'Automne.*

P. J. Redouté pinx. Imprimerie de Rémond. Bessin Sculp.

ROSA CHINENSIS JACQ. CV.

Autumn-flowering Variety of China Rose | Herbstblühende Chinarose | Variété du Rosier de Chine

Rosa Evratina. *Rosier d'Evrat.*

P. J. Redouté pinx. Imprimerie de Rémond Langlois Sculp.

? *ROSA EVRATINA* BOSC

Rosa Rubiginosa Vaillantiana.　　　*L'Eglantine de Vaillant.*

P.J. Redouté pinx.　　　Imprimerie de Rémond.　　　Victor sculp.

? *ROSA MICRANTHA* BORRER VAR. *LACTIFLORA*
— | *Kleinblütige Rose* | *Eglantine de Vaillant* [*]

191

Rosa Muscosa Anemone-flora. *La Mousseuse de la Fleche.*

P. J. Redouté pinx. Imprimerie de Remond Victor Sculp.

ROSA CENTIFOLIA L. VAR. MUSCOSA CV.
Variety of Moss Rose | Moosrosen-Sorte | Variété du Rosier mousseux

Rosa Pomponiana muscosa.   *Le Pompon mousseux.*

P.J. Redouté pinx.   Imprimerie de Rémond   Victor sculp.

ROSA CENTIFOLIA L. 'MOSSY DE MEAUX'

Moss Rose 'Mossy de Meaux' | Bemooste Dijon-Rose | Rosier Pompon mousseux 'De Meaux'

193

Rosa indica fragrans flore simplici.   *Le Bengale thé à fleurs simples.*

P. J. Redouté pinx.   Imprimerie de Rémond.   Victor sculp.

ROSA × ODORATA SWEET CV.

Single variety of Tea Rose | Einfache Teerosen-Sorte | Variété du Rosier à odeur de thé à fleurs simples [28]

Rosa Noisettiana purpurea. *Rosier Noisette à fleurs rouges.*

P. J. Redouté pinx.   Imprimerie de Remond   Langlois sculp.

? ROSA × L'HERITIERANEA THORY

Boursault Rose | Boursault-Rose | Rosier de Boursault [et]

Rosa Canina Burboniana.   *Rosier de l'Ile de Bourbon.*

P.J. Redouté pinx.   Imprimerie de Rémond   Langlois sculp.

ROSA × BORBONIANA N. DESP.

Bourbon Rose | Bourbonrose | Rosier Bourbon

Rosa Pomponia Burgundiaca.　　*Le Pompon de Bourgogne.*

P. J. Redouté pinx.　　　Imprimerie de Rémond　　　Langlois sculp.

ROSA CENTIFOLIA L. 'PARVIFOLIA'

Cabbage Rose 'Burgundian Rose' | Burgunderröschen | Rosier Pompon de Bourgogne

Glossary

ACETUM ROSARUM
see ROSE VINEGAR

ADONIS GARDENS
The gardens of the ancient Greeks, where they grew small rose bushes with beautiful flowers, often in silver containers.

ALPINE ROSE *(Rosa pendulina* L.)
Wild rose from the mountains of southern and central Europe; shrub, approx. 1 m tall, with reddish shoots, often totally smooth-stemmed, with pink to purple flowers.

APOTHECARIES' ROSE *(Rosa gallica* L. *'Officinalis')*
Also called the "Red rose of Lancaster", a variety of the French rose, growing approx. 70 cm tall, with carmine red, semi-double, fragrant flowers; cultivated in France as early as 1310 for its petals, which were dried and crushed to make a medicinal powder.

APPLE ROSE *(Rosa villosa* L.)
Wild rose which occurs throughout Europe up to the Caucasus and into the Middle East; densely branched bush with short shoots, thin, straight prickles and pink flowers; the hips are used commercially.

AQUA ROSARUM
see ROSE WATER

ARCTIC ROSE *(Rosa acicularis* Lindley)
Wild rose, which grows in Arctic regions; thick, soft-bristled stems grow up to only 1m tall, and carry dark red flowers borne singly; rarely used for hybridisation.

ATTAR OF ROSES
see ROSE OIL

AUSTRIAN COPPER ROSE *(Rosa foetida* Herrm. *'Bicolor')*
Came into being as early as the 16th century, possibly as a chance hybrid; it has single flowers, glowing orange on the inside and yellow on the outside; all modern yellow and orange coloured garden roses have this rose in their parentage.

AUSTRIAN YELLOW ROSE *(Rosa foetida* Herrm.)
West Asiatic wild rose; shrub, growing up to 3 m in its native habitat, with deep yellow flowers, which have a disagreeable scent; parent of the yellow- and orange-coloured large-flowered bush roses.

AUTUMN DAMASK ROSE *(Rosa × damascena* Miller var. *semperflorens* G. Rowley)
Garden rose assumed to be a hybrid of the French rose and the Musk rose *(Rosa gallica.* L. × *Rosa moschata* Herrm.); as their common name indicates, these roses can flower twice in a year; an important variety of this rose is known as 'Quatre Saisons', which flowers in the summer, with a second, smaller flush of flowers in the autumn; these roses have been crossed with other roses to produce other repeat-flowering damask roses.

AYRSHIRE ROSES
Garden roses developed from *Rosa arvensis* Hudson at the beginning of the 19th century.

BANKSIAN ROSE *(Rosa banksiae* Aiton fil.)
Chinese wild rose; in its country of origin it climbs to 15 m tall; evergreen, smooth-stemmed shrub with bristly, deciduous auxiliary leaves, with small, fragrant, white or yellow flowers; it has many varieties.

BARBERRY ROSE *(Rosa persica* Michaux)
Wild rose from Asia, occurring on salty soils near the Caspian Sea and the Aral Sea; it has simple leaves, which is why it is categorised as a sub-genus, and yellow flowers with a deep red centre, borne singly; difficult to grow in cultivation.

BEDEGUAR FUNGUS
see ROSE GALLS

BENGAL ROSE
see CHINA ROSE *(Rosa chinensis* Jacq.)

"BLACK ROSE"
There is no really black rose, but some roses are of so deep a red that they can be considered to be black.

BOURBON ROSE *(Rosa × borboniana* N. Desp.)
Garden rose, a hybrid of *Rosa chinensis* Jacq. × *Rosa × damascena* Miller, originating from the Ile du Bourbon (now Réunion); vigorous, remontant. It originally had medium-sized, carmine pink flowers with approx. 20 petals; there are many varieties.

BURNET ROSE *(Rosa pimpinellifolia* L.)
Euro-Asian wild rose of suckering habit with very dense, prickly and bristly branches; has been cultivated for many years; there are many varieties.

BUSH ROSES
Collective term for varieties that form bushy shrubs up to 1m tall with well-branched shoots, usually remontant; the largest group of roses.

CABBAGE ROSE
see PROVENCE ROSE *(Rosa × centifolia* L.)

CAROLINA ROSE *(Rosa carolina* L.)
North American wild rose of suckering habit; sometimes sold in nurseries under the name *Rosa virginiana.*

CHEROKEE ROSE *(Rosa laevigata* Michaux)
Chinese wild rose; vigorous, evergreen climber, usually with only three leaflets; known only in cultivation in Japan.

CHINA ROSE *(Rosa chinensis* Jacq.)
Chinese wild rose; low-growing, erect, almost smooth-stemmed bush with deep red to almost white flowers; the first plants introduced to the west had pink flowers; there are many winter-hardy varieties.

CINNAMON ROSE
see WHITSUNTIDE ROSE *(Rosa majalis* Herrm.)

CLIMBER
Group of climbing roses of erect habit and with strong shoots that climb without the need for support.

CLIMBING ROSES
Roses of the *Synstylae* group, indigenous to south-east Asia; the following are important wild species: *Rosa multiflora* Thunb., *Rosa wichuraiana* Crépin, *Rosa moschata* Herrm. and *Rosa sempervirens* L.

CLUSTER-FLOWERED BUSH ROSES
A rose group created in the 20th century by crossing large-flowered bush roses with polyantha roses; vigorous, bushy habit with flat flower heads and relatively flat flowers in a wide variety of colours.

CONTAINER-GROWN ROSES
Roses sold in plastic pots; they can be planted out any time, in favourable weather.

CULTIVATED ROSE
see GARDEN ROSE

DAMASK ROSE *(Rosa × damascena* Miller*)*
Parentage unknown, but possibly a natural hybrid. There are two types: summer-flowering and autumn-flowering; the typical damask rose grows up to 2 m tall, with very prickly branches and clusters of flowers that are usually strongly scented; has long been cultivated.

DIES ROSARIUS
Roman festival in commemoration of the dead held on 11 May, the rose being a symbol of death.

DOG ROSE *(Rosa canina* L.*)*
Wild rose common throughout Europe, occurring in a great many forms; shrub, 1–3 m tall, with arched branches and sharp thorns, white to pink flowers; medicinal.

DOUBLE ROSE FLOWERS
Term used to describe flowers whose number of petals has been increased by selective breeding; additional petals are modifications of the stamens and pistils; rose flower are either single (5 petals), semi-double (up to 20 petals), double (up to 40 petals) or fully double (more than 40 petals).

DWARF ROSES
see MINIATURE ROSES

EGLANTINE ROSE
see SWEET BRIAR *(Rosa rubiginosa* L.*)*

ENFLEURAGE
Method of obtaining rose oil; a fine, odourless fat is used to extract the oil from the flower petals; the fatty layer is left on the fresh rose petals until it is saturated.

ESSENCE DE ROSE
see ROSE OIL

EVERGREEN ROSE *(Rosa sempervirens* L.*)*
Wild rose from the Mediterranean; evergreen climbing rose with green shoots and red thorns, with large, white, scented flowers.

FAIRY ROSE *(Rosa chinensis* Jacq. 'Minima'*)*
A garden rose also known as Miss Lawrence's rose; attractive multi-stemmed bush, about 20–50 cm tall, with pale pink single or semi-double flowers; long flowering period.

FIELD ROSE *(Rosa arvensis* Hudson*)*
European wild rose; climbing rose, 1–2 m tall, with many small, hooked thorns; it grows in woodland and has white, unscented flowers; see also AYRSHIRE ROSES.

FLORES ROSAE
Trade name for the rose flower petals of the French rose *(Rosa gallica* L.*)*, which are used for medicinal purposes, e. g. as an astringent or to treat diarrhoea.

FLORIBUNDA ROSES
see CLUSTER-FLOWERED BUSH ROSES

FLORIBUNDA-GRANDIFLORA ROSES
see GRANDIFLORA ROSES

FRENCH ROSE *(Rosa gallica* L.*)*
European wild rose, also found in the Middle East; 40–80 cm tall, suckering shrub with pink to red flowers borne singly; very winter-hardy; it has been in cultivation for a very long time and is a predecessor of the garden roses; more than a thousand varieties were in cultivation in the first half of the 19th century.

FRUCTUS CYNOSBATI
Trade name for the fruit of the dog rose *(Rosa canina* L.*)*, rich in vitamins (especially vitamin C) and used for medicinal purposes as a mild astringent and diuretic.

GALLICA ROSES
see FRENCH ROSE *(Rosa gallica* L.*)*

GARDEN ROSES
Also known as cultivated roses; the term is used to describe roses that have been artificially bred from wild plants (wild roses) and are the result of chance or deliberate modifications to the original form; the lowest taxonomic unit of cultivated plants is the variety or cultivar.

GOLDEN ROSE
Traditionally, an honour bestowed by the pope on ruling houses or particularly on individuals who have been of service to the Church; since the 12th century, it has taken the form of a golden rose, blessed by the pope; the award for the best rose of the year, e. g. The Hague (Netherlands), Kortrijk (Belgium) or Orléans (France).

GRANDIFLORA ROSES
Came into being in the 20th century as a result of crossing a large-flowered with a cluster-flowered bush rose; according to international nomenclature rules, the term "grandiflora" may not be used for a rose group, as the name *Rosa grandiflora* has already been used to describe other roses.

GROUNDCOVER ROSES
Collective term for varieties of various habits that are suitable for providing low, spreading greenery, also for container planting and borders; bush roses, usually 15–40 cm tall with small, decorative flowers.

GRASSLAND ROSE *(Rosa agrestis* Savi*)*
European wild rose, also found in north Africa; shrub, 1–2 m tall, with sturdy prickles and pale pink to whitish flowers.

HALF-STANDARD ROSES
Top-grafted roses with a stem height of approx. 60 cm from ground level to the lowest branches; miniature roses and ground-cover roses are usually used as material for half-standards.

HIMALAYAN MUSK ROSE *(Rosa brunonii* Lindley*)*
Wild rose from the Himalaya; vigorous climber with white flowers; frequently cultivated in milder regions.

HIP
Fruit of the rose formed from the receptacle (hypanthium); its vitamin C content is much higher than that of the orange; many garden varieties have lost the ability to form hips and are thus sterile.

HUDSON BAY ROSE *(Rosa blanda* Aiton*)*
North American wild rose; shrub, up to 2 m tall, with nearly thornless stems and 5–7 elliptical leaflets similar to those of the ash tree.

HULTHEMIA Focke
Term used to describe a sub-genus of the genus *Rosa*, characterised by single leaves with no secondary leaves and flowers borne singly, such as, for example, the Barberry rose *(Rosa persica* Michaux*)*.

HYBRID TEA ROSES
see LARGE-FLOWERED BUSH ROSES

JAPANESE ROSE *(Rosa rugosa* Thunb.*)*
Wild rose from temperate north-east Asia, naturalised in parts of Europe and North America; thick stemmed, tomentose, extremely prickly shrub with pink-red flowers, very winter-hardy; there are now many varieties of this rose; it is often planted to stabilise sand dunes.

JAPANESE ROSE *(Rosa multiflora* Thunb.*)*
A wild rose from Japan and Korea, naturalised in the eastern USA; a very vigorous, densely branching climbing rose with white flowers, often used for breeding; there are now many varieties of tall-growing climbing roses.

KAZANLIK ROSE *(Rosa × damascena* Miller 'Trigintipetala'*)*
Oil-producing rose from the Valley of the Roses, named after the industrial town of Kazanlik in the centre of this rose growing area of Bulgaria.

KORDESII CLIMBERS
Climbing roses of garden origin characterised by vigorous growth, resistance to disease, glossy foliage, prolific and long-lasting flowers.

LAMBERTIANA ROSES
Old name for "long-flowering" bush roses produced by crossing the musk rose *(Rosa moschata* Herrm*.)* with *Rosa multiflora* Thunb; large-flowered bush roses; oldest group of roses among the modern garden roses; the first were developed from tea roses crossed with other roses; today more than 6000 varieties have been developed.

MACARTNEY ROSE *(Rosa bracteata* Wendl*.)*
Chinese wild rose, also found in Taiwan, brought back to England in the 18th century by Lord Macartney; erect, evergreen, bushy shrub with large, fragrant, milky white flowers borne singly.

MINIATURE ROSES
Term used to describe smaller versions of taller-growing bush roses; they are usually 15–20 cm tall and bear attractive, small flowers.

MODERN ROSES
Collective term for all garden roses belonging to rose categories which came into being after 1867, in other words after the introduction of the first large-flowered bush roses, as opposed to old garden roses, which were in existence prior to that date; the remontant roses form the link between the two groups; large-flowered and cluster-flowered bush roses, grandiflora roses and polyantha roses belong to this group.

MOSS ROSES
Varieties of the Provence rose *(Rosa × centifolia* L*.)*, whose flower stalks have particularly sticky, fragrant glands; they are called moss roses because of the moss-like growth on the sepals, and also often on the thorns and especially the oil-producing glands.

MUSK ROSE *(Rosa moschata* Herrm*.)*
Origin unknown, possibly the Middle East; shrub of lax habit with reddish, sparsely thorned shoots and white flowers, the petals of which release a strong musk scent; it has been used for many crosses and as a parent of many varieties of shrub roses.

NOISETTE ROSES *(Rosa × noisettiana* Thory*)*
Group of climbing roses produced by crossing the China and musk roses, with yellow, white or pink flowers, sometimes with up to 100 flowers per cluster; only a few varieties have remained in cultivation.

OIL-PRODUCING ROSES
Roses grown for the production of rose oil, for example the damask rose *(Rosa × damascena* Miller*)* in Turkey and Bulgaria (see also Kazanlik rose) and the Provence rose *(Rosa centifolia* L*.)* in France and Morocco.

OLD ROSES
Roses already in existence before 1867, the date when the first large-flowered bush roses were introduced; this category also includes varieties of a later date.

PAESTUM
Ancient centre of rose cultivation, situated south of Naples on the Gulf of Salerno; the rose grown there was possibly the damask rose *(Rosa × damascena* Miller*)*.

PERFOLIATED ROSE
Term used to describe a deformation of rose flowers; a second flower grows up through the first rose flower; botanically, the phenomenon is known as proliferation.

PERNETIANA ROSES
Garden roses produced by hybridising the Austrian yellow rose; as a group they are so susceptible to rust that they disappeared from gardens many years ago, superseded by the modern large-flowered bush roses.

POLYANTHA ROSES
Garden roses, *Rosa polyantha* Sieb. & Zucc. is an earlier, now invalid name for *Rosa multiflora* Thunb. from Japan; in 1870, rose breeders began to cross other roses with this Japanese species and called the varieties so obtained polyantha hybrids or polyantha roses; most varieties available today are very bushy with many flowers and are suitable for massing.

PORTLAND ROSES *(Rosa × damascena* Miller × *Rosa chinensis* Jacq. *semperflorens* Koehne*)*
Group of garden roses used for breeding purposes from 1800 to 1850, as they produced a small, second flush of flowers.

PRAIRIE ROSE *(Rosa setigera* Michaux*)*
American wild rose; shrub, 1–2 m tall, with dark pink flowers, used for breeding winter-hardy climbing roses.

PROVENCE ROSE *(Rosa centifolia* L*.)*
Garden rose of unknown origin; shrub growing to 2 m tall, with protruding pinnatifid sepals and white to deep red, fragrant flowers; a complex hybrid that developed gradually between the 16th and 18th centuries, it has a great many varieties, including moss roses.

RAMBLER ROSES
Group of roses with flexible shoots that require support; they are usually descendants of *Rosa wichuraiana* Crépin.

RED CRIMEAN ROSE
A hybrid of the French and damask rose grown on the Crimea for its oil.

RED ROSE OF LANCASTER
Another name for the Apothecaries' rose and used as the emblem of the House of Lancaster in the Wars of the Roses in England.

REMONTANT ROSES
A rose group, considered to be the link between old and modern garden roses, which came into existence between 1837 and 1890, with all the important garden roses contributing to its development. Remontant roses flower several times in a season; there are many sub-groups, such as Portland roses, remontant Portland hybrids or remontant Bourbon hybrids.

ROBIN'S PINCUSHIONS
see ROSE GALLS

ROSA PHOENICIA BOISS.
Wild rose from Turkey, Syria and the Lebanon; vigorous climbing rose with very long, thin, trailing shoots and large clusters of flowers; the deep roots of this rose make transplanting difficult.

ROSA
The botanical name of the rose genus.

ROSARY
The use of prayer beads, often known as a rosary, to help people with their devotions, has been closely associated with the adoration of the Virgin Mary since the 12th century. As the name suggests, the first rosaries were made from roses.

ROSE DES PEINTRES
see PROVENCE ROSE *(Rosa centifolia* L*.)*

ROSE GALLS
Growths (galls) on the branches of roses, especially the dog rose *(Rosa canina* L*.)*, caused by the sting of the rose gall wasp; in popular medicine, these were used for insomnia and used to be called "Schlafäpfel" (sleeping apples) in German, Robin's pincushions and Bedeguar fungus in English.

ROSE HIP SYRUP
A brownish syrup, similar to raspberry syrup, with a strong rose flavour.

ROSE OF PAESTUM
Probably the damask rose *(Rosa × damascena* Miller*)*; see also PAESTUM.

ROSE OIL
Rose oil is a perfume, a light or dark yellow or greenish, thickish substance, an essential oil that solidifies into a crystalline mass at temperatures below 20°C; it smells strongly of fresh roses.

ROSE RUST
A fungal disease of roses, especially wild roses and roses planted in open ground.

ROSE VINEGAR

Rose buds are collected before they open, then dried and soaked in vinegar; the resultant rose vinegar has been used as a remedy for fatigue and impotence.

ROSE VIRUS 1

A viral disease of roses found today in almost all rose growing areas.

ROSE WATER

Produced from rose petals distilled in water, it is used for medicinal purposes.

ROSEWOOD

The wood from old rootstocks is fine-grained, very solid and beautifully veined, making it highly sought after for inlay work and marquetry; the stems of garden roses are rarely strong enough for this purpose.

SCENTED ROSES

The scent is exuded from tiny glands on the surface of the petals; dark-coloured roses are generally more fragrant than light-coloured ones, and the more petals there are, the stronger the scent.

SCOTCH ROSE

see BURNET ROSE *(Rosa pimpinellifolia* L.*)*

SCOTS ROSE

see BURNET ROSE *(Rosa pimpinellifolia* L.*)*

SEMEN CYNOSBATI

Trade name for the seeds extracted from the hips of dog roses *(Rosa canina* L.*)*, in botanical terms the actual fruits, which can be used for medicinal purposes, e. g. drunk as an infusion for bladder complaints.

SEMI-EVERGREEN CLIMBING ROSE
(Rosa wichuraiana Crépin*)*

East Asiatic wild rose, naturalised in North America; with stems 2–5 m long and often trailing, with leaves that are shiny on both sides and white, fragrant flowers in spherical panicles; parent of many varieties of climbing rose; used on graves in North America ("Memorial rose").

SHRUB ROSES

A group of roses of bushy habit, with erect, occasionally also arching stems; this group includes the old roses as well as the modern, remontant shrub roses.

SILK ROSE *(Rosa sericea* Lindley*)*

Wild rose from the Himalayas; a very erect, vigorous shrub, the undersides of the leaves being covered with silky hairs; the white flowers usually have only four petals, not the usual five.

SINGLE ROSE FLOWERS

Term used to describe rose flowers with only five (occasionally four) petals, as they typically occur in wild roses.

SLATER'S CRIMSON CHINA ROSE
(Rosa chinensis Jacq. var. *semperflorens* Koehne*)*

Garden rose, originally from India; attractive bush with thin shoots and deep red, semi-double, fragrant flowers and a particularly long flowering period; all deep red roses are descended from this rose.

SPORT

Term used to describe a mutation, i. e. a deviation in genotype, that occurs spontaneously and changes the external features of a rose.

STANDARD ROSES

Top-grafted roses with a stem height of approx. 90 cm from ground level to the lowest branches; cluster-flowered and large-flowered bush roses are most commonly used to make standards.

"SUB ROSA"

The rose as emblem of secrecy; "sub rosa" agreements are confidential and commit the participants to secrecy; thus roses were carved in wood or stone on confessional boxes to symbolise the sacred nature of the seal of confession.

SULPHUR ROSE *(Rosa hemisphaerica* Herrm.*)*
Not found in the wild; a bush, 1–2 m tall, with very erect branches and sulphur yellow, scentless flowers.

SUMMER DAMASK ROSES

Garden roses, possibly a hybrid of the French rose *(R. gallica* L.*)* and *R. phoenicia* Boiss; as their name indicates, these damask roses flower only in summer.

SWEET BRIAR *(Rosa rubiginosa* L.*)*
A European species; very vigorous, thorny shrub with leaves that smell strongly of apples when wet. It has been in cultivation since 1600 and is frequently used for hybridisation.

TEA ROSE *(Rosa × odorata* Sweet*)*
Cultivated rose from China; evergreen climbing rose with long shoots and white, pale pink or yellowish flowers; the scent produced by crushing the leaves or flowers is said to have been reminiscent of tealeaves. There used to be a great many varieties.

TOMENTOSE ROSE *(Rosa tomentosa* Smith*)*
Wild rose that can be found across Europe through to the Caucasus and the Middle East; shrub, 2 m tall, with thick, straight or arched thorns.

TRAILING DOG ROSE

see FIELD ROSE *(Rosa arvensis* Hudson*)*

TUDOR ROSE

English heraldic rose, depicted as two roses, one inside the other, the outer rose being red, the inner white.

VARIETY

Term for a group of cultivated plants that can be identified by particular usually morphological features, which it retains when reproduced vegetatively.

VIRGINIA ROSE *(Rosa virginiana* Miller*)*
North American wild rose; approx. 1.5 m tall bush with glossy green leaves and pale pink flowers.

WHITE ROSE OF YORK *(Rosa × alba* L.*)*
Probably a natural hybrid, it has been cultivated since Classical times; shrub, growing up to 2 m tall, with white to soft pink, mainly semi-double or double flowers; there are many varieties of this rose.

WHITSUNTIDE ROSE *(Rosa majalis* Herrm.*)*
Eurasian wild rose; shrub with suckers produced from below ground level and carmine red flowers with slightly toothed petals; cultivated since before 1600.

WILD ROSES

Wild and their descendants that occur naturally in the wild; they always have single flowers.

YORK AND LANCASTER ROSE
(Rosa × damascena Miller 'Versicolor')
Shrub rose growing up to approx; 1m tall, with white-haired leaves and loosely double flowers that can be white or pink (both colours occurring simultaneously on the same plant); flowers that are half white and half pink (but never striped) can also appear. It gets its name from the two feuding houses in the English War of the Roses, but came into existence much later.

Index

Bibliography

On the life and work of Redouté

BLUNT, W. & STEARN, W. T.,
The Art of Botanical Illustration, The Royal Botanic Gardens, Kew 1994.

DELCOURT, R. & LAWALREE, R.,
»Pierre-Joseph Redouté. Botaniste Illustrateur«, in: *Lejeunia*, 13, 1949, 5–20.

LACK, H. W. & BAER, W.,
»Ein botanisches Porzellanservice aus Berlin für Kaiserin Joséphine«, in: *Willdenowia*, 1978, 8, 235–259.

LÉGER, C.,
Redouté et son temps, Paris 1945.

MANNERING, E.,
Pierre-Joseph Redouté. Rosen, Stuttgart 1954.

STAFLEU, F. A.,
»Pierre-Joseph Redouté«, in: *DSB XI.*, New York 1975.

STAFLEU, F. A.,
»Redouté – Peintre de Fleurs«, in: LAWRENCE, G. H. M. (ed.), *A Catalogue of Redouteana*, Pittsburgh 1963.

VOS, DE A.,
»Biographie de P. J. Redouté 1759–1840«, in: *Belgique horticole*, 1873.

Botany and horticulture

HESS, H. E., LANDOLT, E. & HIRZEL, R.,
Flora der Schweiz und angrenzender Gebiete, Vol. 2, Basel 1977.

HEYWOOD, V. H. (ED.),
Blütenpflanzen der Welt, Basel 1982.

KRÄTZ, O.,
Goethe und die Naturwissenschaften, Munich 1992.

KRÜSSMANN, G.,
Handbuch der Laubgehölze, Vol. III, Berlin 1978.

KRÜSSMANN, G.,
Rosen, Rosen, Rosen: unser Wissen über die Rose, Berlin/Hamburg 1986.

LACK, E. & LACK, H. W.,
Botanik und Gartenbau in Prachtwerken, Berlin/Hamburg 1985.

MÄGDEFRAU, K.,
Paläobiologie der Pflanzen, 4. ed., Stuttgart/Jena 1964.

MÄGDEFRAU, K.,
Geschichte der Botanik. Leben und Leistung großer Forscher, 2. ed., Stuttgart/Jena/New York 1992.

MARZELL, H.,
Wörterbuch der deutschen Pflanzennamen, Vol. III, 1977.

NAKAMURA, T.,
Kinmôzui, 2. ed. (Reprint 1976), Tokyo 1666.

NISSEN, C.,
Botanische Prachtwerke. Die Blütezeit der Pflanzenillustration von 1740 bis 1840, Vienna 1933.

NISSEN, C.,
Die botanische Buchillustration, ihre Geschichte und Bibliographie, 2. ed., Stuttgart 1966.

MEUSEL, H., JÄGER, E. & WEINERT, E.,
Vergleichende Chronologie der zentraleuropäischen Flora, Vol. 1: Text, Vol. 2: Maps, Jena 1965.

SCHNEEBELI-GRAF, R.,
Blütenland China, Vol. I: Ornamental plants, Vol. II: Useful and medicinal plants, 2. ed., Basel/Boston/Berlin 1995.

SCHUBERT, R. & WAGNER, G.,
Botanisches Wörterbuch. Pflanzennamen und botanische Fachwörter, 10. ed., Stuttgart 1991.

SCHUSTER, J.,
Goethe, Die Metamorphose der Pflanzen, Berlin 1924.

TUTIN, T. G. & AL.,
Flora Europaea, Vol. III, Cambridge 1968.

WISSOWA, G. & KROLL, W.,
Paulys Real-Enzyclopädie der classischen Altertumswissenschaft, 13. Vol., Stuttgart 1910.

ZANDER, R.,
Handwörterbuch der Pflanzennamen. Edited by: ENCKE, F., BUCHHEIM, G. & SEYBOLD, S., 15. ed., corrected reprint of the 14. ed., Stuttgart 1994.

Medicine

GARBERS, K., *KITAB KIMIYA'AL-'ITR WAT-TAS'IDAT.*
Buch über die Chemie des Parfüms und die Destillationen von YA'QUB B. ISHAQ AL-KINDI. Ein Beitrag zur Geschichte der arabischen Parfümchemie und Drogenkunde aus dem 9. Jahrhundert, p. C., Leipzig 1948.

HOPPE, H. A.,
Taschenatlas der Drogenkunde, Berlin/New York 1981.

LEUNG, A. Y.,
Chinesische Heilkräuter, Cologne 1985.

MOSIG, A. & SCHRAMM, G.,
Der Arzneipflanzen- und Drogenschatz Chinas und die Bedeutung des Pen, .Ts'ao Kang Mu als Standardwerk der Chinesischen Materia Medica, Berlin 1955.

MÜLLER, I.,
Die pflanzlichen Heilkräuter bei Hildegard von Bingen, Salzburg 1982.

OHLOFF, G.,
Irdische Düfte. Himmlische Lust. Eine Kulturgeschichte der Duftstoffe, Basel/Boston/Berlin 1992.

SCHNEIDER, W.,
Lexikon zur Arzneimittelgeschichte. Sachwörterbuch zur Geschichte der pharmazeutischen Botanik, Chemie, Mineralogie, Pharmakologie, Zoologie, Vol. 1–7, Frankfurt a. M. 1968–1975.

SCHÖPF, H.,
Zauberkräuter, Wiesbaden 1986.

WOENIG, F.,
Die Pflanzen im alten Ägypten, Leipzig 1886.

Art

BAUMANN, H.,
Die griechische Pflanzenwelt in Mythos, Kunst und Literatur, Munich 1982.

HOPPE, B.,
»Darstellung der Alchemie in Gemälden von Jan Brueghel d. Ä. (1568–1625)«, in: *Deutsche Apotheker Zeitung*, 35, 1983, 144–149.

KIRSCHBAUM, E., (ED.),
Lexikon der christlichen Ikonographie, Vol. III, Rome/Freiburg/Basel/Vienna 1971.

SCHMIDT, H.,
Die vergessene Bildersprache christlicher Kunst, 3. ed., Munich 1984.

Acknowledgements

The copy used for printing belongs to the manuscript department of the university library in Erlangen-Nuremberg. We thank the libraries' employees for their friendly assistance. Thanks is due to Brigitte Hoppe for her cooperation and to Otto Bünemann for checking, completing and translating the rose names and the botanical details.

Photographic Credits

Photographs by Kurt Henseler, Tübingen

For the reproduction of the plates on pages 85, 86, 137, 149, 168, 170, 181 and 186 the volumes belonging to the manuscript department of the university library in Tübingen were used. The reproduction of the plate on page 42 was made possible courtesy of the state library in Darmstadt.

© Archiv für Kunst und Geschichte, Berlin: ill. 10, 11, 12
The reproduction of illustration 2 was taken from the book *Georg Krüssmann, Rosen, Rosen, Rosen* (Berlin, 1986) p. 12 with the permission of the Parey Buchverlag in the Blackwell Wissenschafts-Verlag, Berlin.

The legends for the illustration plates contain first the botanical term and then popularly used names in English, German and French, if they were able to be determined. The signs at the end refer to the origin: as a wild rose (✤), as garden rose in culture today (✤), not in culture today (✤).

© 2007   TASCHEN GmbH, Hohenzollernring 53, D-50672 Köln
www.taschen.com
Original edition: © 1999 Benedikt Taschen Verlag GmbH

Editing   Petra Lamers-Schütze, Ines Dickmann, Cologne
Botanical editing   Otto Bünemann, Herdecke; Petra-Andrea Hinz, Aying
Design   Lambert und Lambert, Düsseldorf
Production   Thomas Grell, Cologne
English translation   Lenore M. Dickinson, Cambridge, MA (Barbara Schulz), Harriet Horsfield in association with First Edition Translations Ltd., Cambridge, UK (Petra-Andrea Hinz)

ISBN 978-3-8228-3810-5
Printed in China